Your Emotional Boat
A Field Guide

Linda Branham M.Ed.

authorHOUSE®

AuthorHouse™
1663 Liberty Drive, Suite 200
Bloomington, IN 47403
www.authorhouse.com
Phone: 1-800-839-8640

First published by AuthorHouse 9/16/2008

ISBN: 978-1-4343-6296-4 (sc)

Printed in the United States of America
Bloomington, Indiana

This book is printed on acid-free paper.

Table of Contents

Introduction

This is a Personality Style Inventory to help you assess your personality. It will also help you identify the characteristics of your personality in such a manner that you will understand how to utilize your own strengths and overcome your weaknesses to make the changes in your life that you would like to make.

But do not allow yourself to believe that because you tend toward one type of characteristics, it means you do not possess the other characteristics. For example, not all of us are meant to be detail-oriented. Not all of us are meant to see the big picture. It takes all of us working together to build a meaningful whole. And in having made that statement, please remember that just because details are not your strongest area, it does not mean that you cannot focus on details. It just means that you have to work harder at the details than someone to whom details are their strongest ability.

Section 1
Myers-Briggs Personality Type Indicator

I have connected the personality styles from the Myers-Briggs Type Inventory (MBTI) to boat "styles." If you are interested in a more complete evaluation of your personality style, I recommend that you either contact a psychologist in your area for the complete Myers-Briggs testing, or take the tests in either *Please Understand Me II* by David Keirsey or *Personality Type: An Owner's Manual* by Lenore Thomson. There are also several free tests on the Internet. But for a brief version of the personality test, answer the following questions.

The MBTI psychological types are represented by opposing type preferences. They are as follows:

Primary attitude: where you get your energy and where you direct it. Do you get your energy from being with people or from being alone?

E or I

    1.) When you have a task to complete, you prefer to work on the task:

        a)   _____with a group of friends

b) _____by yourself

2.) When you are "homebound" for some reason, you

    a) _____ wonder what everybody else is doing and what you are missing

    b) _____ enjoy getting to spend some time alone

3.) When you are in a group of people, you

    a) _____ focus your attention on everything that is going on around you, taking in all of the details—sights, sounds, smells

    b) _____ focus your attention one particular item and tune out what everybody else is doing

4.) With your friendships, you are more likely to be the one to

    a.) _____ seek out activities with your friends

    b.) _____ wait for them to seek you out

5.) In conversations with your friends, you find that you prefer to

    a) _____ jump from topic to topic

    b) _____ talk deeply about one particular topic at a time

Write down your number of a's _____ b's _____

If you have more a's than b's, you are an **E**.

If you have more b's, then you are an **I**.

Write this letter in the first space below.

Do you have more **E** characteristics or **I** characteristics? You will probably be mixed in E and I answers, but find that you have more of one side than the other. For example, I am an introvert, but I do talk a lot, which is an E quality. I usually think, then talk; I am usually calm; I like to be alone; I seldom initiate contact with others; I usually think things through, then act; I love to focus completely on a project; and I love to study topics in great detail. Notice that I said "usually," because there are times when that is not the case; but under regular circumstances, those things are true of me. When I write an e-mail to someone, I may take an hour to word it properly before it says what I want it to say. Communication is not an "automatic" process.

Determine your preferences, and decide if you are more like an "E" or an "I."

E _____   or   I _____

If you find it difficult to determine whether you are an E or an I, think about how much action and commotion you need in order to feel comfortable. Extraverts need activity, an outer focus, in order to stay interested; Introverts, on the other hand, become burned out with too much activity. Introverts can lose themselves in a project for long periods of time, feeling stimulated and energized by inner focus, meditation or absorption. Whereas, an Extrovert will get bored with these inner focused projects and feel worn out; they need to get up and interact with others in order to recover their energy.

Remember, each of these personality types is on a continuum, meaning that you may incorporate some characteristics of both personality types. What we are looking for here is how you are most likely to act or think in these situations.

This section is about your approach to life and how you take in information:

S for Sensory (Expressive)
N for Intuitive (Introspective)

1.) When you look at an object (a painting, for example), you

a) _____ notice all of the rich colors and textures, focusing on how they blend together

b) _____ notice and think about how the painting was made, how it reminds you of something else

2.) When you are trying to make a particular point during a conversation, you

a) _____ make your point in a sequential manner, where one point follows another in order. Find that you are direct and to the point.

b) _____ make your point by jumping from one idea to the next in random order as one thought leads you to another idea. Find that you repeat points, rephrase, and seem to make a lot of twists and turns along the way.

3.) You would describe yourself as more

a) _____ down-to-earth and sensible

b) _____ imaginative and creative

4.) When making decisions about your life, you are

a) _____ more comfortable with the familiar, what is known

b) _____ attracted to things that are unusual, new, or different

5.) You are more concerned with

  a) _____ details and facts about how to go about making something work; just want to "*do it*"

  b) _____ looking at the big picture and what is possible; thinking of all the potential ways that you can come up with to make it work

Count the number of a's and b's. If you have more a's, then you are a Sensor. If you have more b's, then you are an Intuitive.

S_____   or   N _____

Write your preference in the second space.

If you find it difficult to determine whether you are an S or an N, think about how you react when you encounter an unusual circumstance, something out of the ordinary. A Sensate will focus on the details, the facts, the direct experience. The Intuitive will focus on the *meaning* of the unusual circumstance; in fact they can focus on the meaning and the potential to such a degree that they may overlook the facts and details.

Next is how you make decisions or come to conclusions:

T for Thinking (Logical)
F for Feeling (Emotional)

  1.) When you have to make a choice about something in your life, you are more comfortable

  a) _____ coming to the final decision, finding it a relief when the choice is made and completed.

  b) _____ knowing that the process is still open and you are looking for options.

2.) Which would best describe your choice-making process?

    a) _____ Make a list of pros and cons, a logical, cool-headed approach.

    b) ____ Consider your feelings about the issue and how it will affect everyone.

3.) Which would be your greatest priority in determining your choice?

    a) _____ How the decision will work.

    b) _____ How people will feel.

4.) People would describe you as

    a) _____ just, fair, and impartial

    b) _____ merciful, caring, and sensitive

5.) When presented with a new idea, you would describe yourself as

    a) _____ skeptical and questioning

    b) _____ accepting and open

Which style are you more likely to use when making a decision?

Number of a's _____

Number of b's _____

If more a's, then you are T—Thinking or Logically oriented.

If more b's, then you are F—Feeling or Emotionally oriented.

T _____ or F _____

If you find it difficult to determine whether you are a Thinker or a Feeler think about how you make decisions so that life makes sense to you. A Thinker makes decisions based on impersonal facts, rules, laws, logic or sequential information. A Feeler makes decisions according to his personal beliefs and values, relationships, loyalty, and responsibility to others.

Finally, in this section we look at "How you organize your world and live life."

J for Judging (Scheduling)
P for Perceiving (Probing)

1.) You would describe yourself as

    a) _____ organized

    b) _____ adaptable

2.) In your office and living space you are

    a.) _____ well-organized, with a place for everything

    b.) _____ messy and cluttered, often have trouble finding things

3.) In defining how you prefer to live your life:

    a) _____ you prefer having rules, structure, and guidelines to live by; you find that they bring stability and security

    b) _____ you feel that rules are restrictions on your freedom and creativity, preferring to take things as they come.

4.) In the regular scheme of things, you

    a.) _____ prefer to have specific plans to follow

    b.) _____ prefer to leave options open and be flexible

5.) How do you approach the goals in your life?

    a.) _____ You are more likely to stick with a goal. You are likely to set and be driven to reach that goal.

    b.) _____ You are likely to change goals midway and improvise, finding other options. You prefer the starting of a task rather than the completing of it.

Again, count your number of a's and b's.

a's are J Judging/Scheduling

b's are P (Perceiving)

J _____ or P _____

If you find it difficult to determine whether you are a Judger or a Perceiver think about how you approach the world. A Judger/Scheduler approaches the world by thinking about the possibilities and preparing for them; they like to organize their lives so that they are ready for anything that may occur. Perceivers are more flexible, preferring to keep their options open and taking life as it happens; in fact Perceivers will often resist schedules and organization.

Now, write down your one letter from each preference above;

E___ I___ ;   S___ N___;   T___ F___;   J___ P___

This would be your style. For example I am an INFP; my daughter, Sarah, is an ENFP; my son, Joshua, is an ESFP; and my oldest daughter, Dina, is an ISFP.

There are sixteen possible combinations of the above letters.

ESTP   ISTP   ESFP   ISFP

ESTJ   ISTJ   ESFJ   ISFJ

ENFJ   INFJ   ENFP   INFP

ENTJ   INTJ   ENTP   INTP

David Keirsey later separated those sixteen types into four main groups: the SPs, SJs, NFs, and NTs.

Even though we are one personality style, which we use throughout our entire lives, there are circumstances where we learn to use characteristics that are not our preferred pattern of interacting. I think one of the traps of using these types of labels on ourselves is that we use it as an excuse not to be able to do something; it becomes a limiting factor. These are only are preferred ways of interacting. We can all do the other parts that are not our preferred way, but we have to work harder to do them. For example, being an INFP, I find that meeting deadlines and sticking to details is not my preferred way of being. But I can, and do, manage these things. It just takes more effort on my part than it would someone who is an ISTJ, because they thrive on organization and deadlines.

Another good example is my daughter, Sarah. Sarah has a muscle in her right leg that does not work properly, and so as a child, had to wear a leg brace. The doctors believe she may have contracted polio from the vaccine as an infant. I taught her that even though she had this problem, there was nothing the other children did that she couldn't do, but she was just going to have to work harder at it. In fact, her dad had an article published in *Chicken Soup for the Soul* about this issue.

A Lesson in Heart

A lesson in "heart" is my little, 10-year-old daughter, Sarah,
who was born with a muscle missing in her foot
and wears a brace all the time. She came home one beautiful
spring day to tell me she had competed in "field day."
That's where they have lots of races and other competitive events.
Because of her leg support, my mind raced as I tried to think
of encouragement for my Sarah, things I could say to her
about not letting this get her down—but before I
could get a word out, she said, "Daddy, I won two of the races!"
I couldn't believe it! And then Sarah said,
"I had an advantage." Ahh. I knew it.
I thought she must have been given a head start...
some kind of physical advantage. But again, before I could
say anything, she said, "Daddy, I didn't get a head start...
My advantage was I had to try harder!"

~Stan Frager~

When I read this story that Stan had published, I felt very proud that she had listened and understood what I was trying to tell her.

So remember the lesson of this story, you can do *all* of the skills and ways of being, but if it is not your preferred way, you will need to "work harder at it."

Also, your place on the continuum of each style will influence your personality style. Again, using myself as an example, I am an INFP. I am strong in the I, N and P areas, but closer to the middle in the F (Feeling) area. This means that even though I tend to make decisions based on my relationships, values and beliefs, I also bring in the logical aspects of the situation. I am influenced by an emotional appeal, but not overcome by it.

Since we are using boats to represent our personalities in this book, I have used a boat to represent each Myers-Briggs personality style. As you read the "boat" styles, try to determine how they fit into your life.

As you read, if you discover that the description of your style does not fit you, go back to the questions above and see if you can determine where a different letter may be better suited. For example, you may have had almost an equal number of answers in a category, but the one with lesser answers was more important.

Another qualifying piece of information is that in researching the personality styles, several researchers listed well-known people as representing specific personality styles. I have no way of verifying that the well-known person is actually that personality style. The quotes given are statements that would represent a person with that particular personality style, whether the person is actually that personality style or not.

Section 2
Putting the Information to use

Now that you have an awareness of which traits you possess, what does it mean? And how can you use it in your daily life? I want to give you a little bit of information about the meanings of the terms and your score from the test above.

(E) EXTRAVERSION or (I) INTROVERSION

This category refers to your general approach to life, how you define yourself, where you get your energy.

E's are concentrated outside of themselves, in the world around them. Their identity is very much connected to the outside world—what others can see and respond to. They tend to judge themselves by the opinions and values of others. They get their energy from the people and things outside of themselves; they focus outside of themselves to gain energy and "recharge their batteries."

I's, on the other hand, classify things in the environment by their own understanding and values. They form an opinion of who they are by judging themselves against their own views, impressions, and beliefs. They focus inward to gain energy and may find they need to be alone in order to "recharge their batteries."

In *Personality Type*, Lenore Thompson says that Extraverts say "Yes too soon, and no too late," whereas Introverts tend to say "No too soon, and yes too late."

When a person is standing in front of you that you want to be able to communicate with and connect to, how do you know if they are an E or an I?

Indications:

E's	I's
Jump from topic to topic	Like in-depth discussions
Scan their environment	Focus inward
Answer questions quickly	Pause and reflect before answering
Prefer several tasks all at once	Prefer to concentrate on one thing at a time
Like to be around people	Like to spend time alone
Need external stimulation	Need time for internal focus
Have many interests and friends	Have fewer in-depth interests and have a few very close friends.
Enthusiastic and outgoing	calmer and self-contained
Act quickly under stress	may slow down under stress

Once you have determined that the person in front of you is an E or an I, how do you communicate with them in order to connect more effectively?

How to communicate effectively with an Extravert:

Let them talk and think out loud.

Many of them like to "talk to themselves." This is very true of my office assistant, Marietta. She carries on conversations with herself on a regular basis. We have now learned to ask if she is talking to us or to herself.

Have several different topics handy, touch on each one quickly, and then move on to something else.

No long discussions about a specific topic; they will have tuned you out and moved on to checking out the environment. So brief pieces of information, please.

Extraverts will maintain eye contact when they are speaking, but when they listen, they will start scanning their surroundings and getting in touch with what is going on around them.

I will discuss this more in the Introvert section.

Remember that they respond quickly to questions and outward events.

They are wonderful on game shows and debates that require quick responses.

During times of stress or crisis, Extraverts need to talk it out. So if you are in a helping profession, these are the people who need to talk, and love group support. They respond to activities and find security in the things and people around them.

Also remember that Extraverts require an outward focus in order to stay involved and connected. They can become restless and lose interest when there is not enough external stimulation and activity. In a dire crisis like a hurricane or tornado, when an extravert suffers huge losses, they need to stay outwardly focused and busy. They need to be connected to friends and other people. It is essential that they be able to talk about the experience. It is fundamental to their natures that they reaffirm their identity in light of the things they have lost.

How to communicate effectively with an Introvert:

Ask them questions, then pause and give them time to respond. Listen carefully when they do respond.

> As an introvert myself, I have found that many times I have a response to a topic long after the subject has been changed by my coworkers. Sometimes I bring up the topic again, but usually I just let it go and do not give my opinion.

Talk about one topic at a time, going in depth about that topic before moving on to something else.

> Introverts can have a difficult time jumping from topic to topic because it takes them longer to respond. They have that extra step of having to relate the information to their values and beliefs before they speak up.
>
> Many times extraverts will think that a topic has been agreed upon, or that there are no questions, when in truth the introvert is still processing the information.
>
> During group discussions, they will tend to sit back and listen, not because they are not listening or don't have any ideas, but because they need to reflect and internalize the information before speaking. Also, they do not like to interrupt their talkative extraverted associates, who always seem to have a quick response.

Don't interrupt an introvert when they are speaking, because they may have a difficult time picking up where they left off.

Introverts can sometimes communicate better in writing, where they have time to organize their thoughts internally. Remember that Introverts tend to lessen eye contact when speaking in order

to internally focus on what they want to say, and then increase eye contact when listening in order to focus on taking in the information

> This is opposite of the extravert. This can cause both Introverts **and** Extroverts to believe that the other is not interested or not listening, when in actuality, they are just processing information according to the way their brain functions.

Remember that they may think they have told you something, when they haven't.

> This happens because they have rehearsed the conversation internally so many times that they believe they have actually had the conversation.

Again, they need time to internalize the information before they respond, which makes them not as effective on game shows as the extraverts mentioned above. Not because they don't know the information or because their memories are not as good, but because their thinking processes require that extra step of going inside and connecting the information to their internal thought processes.

If you are in a helping profession and working with an introvert, ask a question to draw them out, but then sit back and allow them time to reflect and process before they answer. Having an introvert journal or write down their thoughts can be a helpful way to get them to become more aware of, and connected to, their own internal reactions.

Since introverts are constantly processing the external world by relating to it internally, they can quickly become over-stimulated when many things are occurring at once. During times of extreme crisis, they need to quietly process the information and relate it internally to their own view of the world before they can talk about it coherently. They need to be drawn out eventually, but after they have had time to assess the events internally.

S (SENSING)   or   N (INTUITING)

Sensing and Intuiting refer to the way that a person processes new information or experiences. When an S is presented with a new idea, they will relate it to a past experience and gather all of the facts from A to Z, one step at a time. They need a direct sensory experience, combined with facts and details, in order to develop a firm understanding. Their surroundings have a direct impact upon them, and they pay attention to what they are able to take in through their five senses.

An N will process the new information or experience by imagining all of its possibilities for the future, and may make huge leaps in getting insights and possibilities with just a few pertinent facts. They ignore the material surface of things, what they can take in with their five senses, and take leaps into the possibilities and the overall picture. They are not interested in the facts or details. They are interested in the insights, connections, and meanings.

How do you determine if the person in front of you is an S (Sensor) or an N (Intuitive)?

Indications:

S	N
Past experiences	Future-oriented
Literal	Originality and alternate meaning (metaphors)
Rely on the five senses	Rely on "gut" feeling
Common sense	Insight
Interested in "real" things that are useful	Interested in ideas and concepts
Pragmatic and precise	Inspired and enthusiastic
Interested in life as it exists right now	Invested in future possibilities

Interested in security of material reality	Fascination with the unknown
Need to know all the facts before deciding	Tend to get the "whole picture" with a few facts
Reliance on past experience in solving problems	Reliance on ingenuity when solving problems
Highly observant	Aware of patterns and "gut" reactions
Need sensory evidence in order to believe	Need new possibilities in order to become motivated
Sense of identity in possessing and having and using things	Some resistance to material possessions as being possibly restricting

How to communicate effectively with an S:

Remember that S's like to talk in an uncomplicated and straightforward manner; they get right to the point.

No idle chit-chat for them—they want to discuss the topic at hand.

Prepare facts ahead of time and have examples ready for them.

If you are not prepared to back up your point with facts and details, they will quickly lose interest or consider your viewpoint invalid. They need to be shown why and how your viewpoint is correct.

Talk in complete sentences.

Incomplete sentences mean incomplete information to them. They may be asking themselves if you are not completing the sentence because you do not know the information.

Emphasize the practical applications of what you are saying.

> How is this important? What is its benefit? How can they use the information you are telling them? These are the questions an S wants to have answered.

When attempting to convince them of your point of view or of a new idea, illustrate your points with past and real experiences.

> If you can give them examples of how this was helpful in the past, they will consider your point of view to be more convincing or your information to be more legitimate. If you can relate your information or idea to something in their past that they can relate to, they will be even more likely to believe and take seriously what you are saying.

Present your information with step-by-step points.

> S's are systematic and go from A to B to C—they don't want to skip over points. Numbering the points is helpful.

Give them concrete and practical ideas.

> Talk about what they can observe, sense, touch, hear. Let them know how they can "use" the information that you are talking to them about.

If you are in a helping profession and an S experiences a crisis in life, they need to be reminded of past situations when they were able to overcome obstacles. They need assistance in working out a detailed, step-by-step plan that will help them overcome whatever the situation is. Since they are deeply influenced by what they see and hear around them, it is important for them to know what they can do "now" to get started. Having a direct experience of stability is important to them—for example, holding an item that has meaning to them, or being involved in the process of cooking a meal. It is essential that they have the direct experience of something that is concrete and practical, a task that requires a step-by-step course of action. This will assist them in being in the present (the here and now) and connect them to the material world via their senses.

How to communicate effectively with an N:

For goodness' sakes, talk about the possibilities, and what *could* be.

> N's are future-oriented and want to know about the possibilities.

Use lots of analogies and metaphors.

> This will help engage their imagination and get them actively focused on what you are saying.

Try to engage their imagination in the process.

> Get them thinking about the possibilities and what could be. You will lose them if you bog them down with details.

Stay away from a step-by-step description of what you are saying.

> They will already have come to their own conclusion before you can get to the second step. They like to imagine the future possibilities, and they like to create new ways of doing things. Getting bogged down with details of something that is already planned is one sure way to lose their interest.

Ask them to brainstorm options in a situation.

> Asking their views or how they imagine something is one way to get them interested and involved.

If you are in a helping profession and are working with an N during a crisis situation, it would be useful to approach their imagination by getting them to brainstorm ideas of what they *could* do. You may have to suggest an idea or two, but then step back and let their own imagination go to work. Help them see the possibilities for change in their situation, that it is an opportunity for them to create something new. Help them to focus on their options and possibilities.

T (THINKING)   or   F (FEELING)

Thinking and feeling are the way that we organize familiar facts or experiences so that they are predictable and can be understood in a coherent manner. This is how we make our decisions about our lives and what we believe are the most efficient ways for us to live those lives. Thinking and Feeling are not a question of reason versus emotion. They are more concerned with whether a person focuses on logic, impersonal information, and facts, or whether the person is focused on their personal code of values, morals, and ideals.

If a person is standing in front of you, how do you determine if they are a T or an F?

Indications:

T	F
Make decisions impersonally, based on logic and analysis	Make decisions based on shared values, feelings, and relationship
Seem distant towards others	Friendlier towards others
Firm but fair	Empathize, make exceptions
Can be blunt and tactless	Are diplomatic
Cause and effect reasoning	Their needs and needs of others
Give praise sparingly	Give praise often
Rely on justice and fairness	Rely on values and morality
An interest in how things work	Interest in how people feel

Interested in sequence—one step leading to the next	Good sense of how something was said and why
Like to debate or argue	Avoid conflict and disagreements
Find solutions in impartial manner	Find solutions by considering the effects on others
Logical	Sympathetic
Value truth over feelings	Value feelings over truth
Look for points of difference	Look for points of agreement

One way to determine if a person is a Thinker or a Feeler is to ask him how he feels about something. A Thinker will usually say something like "What do you mean, how do I feel? It either is or isn't, its not about feeling!" On the other hand, a Feeler will easily relate their feelings about the topic.

How to communicate effectively with a Thinker:

Be organized and logical, and have your information prepared sequentially ahead of time.

> This sounds similar to an S, but the purpose is different. The T wants logic and truth, whereas an S is interested in fitting the information into their past experience.

Focus on the consequences of whatever your topic is to be.

> What do you want to happen, and why is it beneficial?

Ask them what they think about something, not how they feel about it.

> T's base their decisions on facts, not on feelings.

Remember that Thinkers like to break their conversations down into the number of points being made.

Say things like "The three reasons why we need to plan ahead of time are…." This way, if you can refer to the item being talked about as "Point number 2," for example, you will have scored points with the Thinker.

Don't use personal appeals.

Be objective. Base your conversation on the consequences of actions. Stay calm and unemotional, presenting logical ideas and reasoning.

If you are a helping professional working with a Thinker during a crisis, your approach should appeal to their logical and rational perspective. Rational logic will keep them grounded and effective in approaching the situation. Eventually they will need to access their emotions regarding the situation, but logic, facts, and figures will strengthen them in order to help them make the decisions that they need to make. It will give them a sense of control and continuity.

How to communicate effectively with a Feeler:

Acknowledge and validate their feelings.

Smile frequently, maintain eye contact, and show that you appreciate their hard work and input into whatever the topic is. Be considerate and friendly, showing warmth and caring.

At the very beginning, mention the points where you both agree in order to make the connection with the person.

An F likes to feel a connection with people during conversations. They like to know that there is a sense of respect and equality between the people having the discussion.

When there is disagreement, use a statement like "I'm not sure I understood that correctly, but…"

> This is a way of softening a critical remark or area of disagreement. F's do not like conflict.

If you are a helping professional dealing with a Feeler in a time of crisis, you can assist the person by helping them make decisions based on their feelings and values about relationships with others. Many times a Feeler will get involved in assisting other people as a way of dealing with their own crises. Remember, for a Feeler, feelings are the way they organize familiar facts or experiences in order to form stability and predictability in their lives.

J (JUDGING) or P (PERCEIVING)

J and P describe the ways that people organize their world and how they deal with external reality. I believe that instead of "Judging," a "J" should be described as Structured. J's like to have their lives structured, organized, and planned. They want to make decisions, accomplish goals, and organize everything. P's, on the other hand, like to keep their options open and go with the flow; in fact, they may even rebel against too many plans and organization.

So how do you know if you are face-to-face with a J or P?

Indications:

J	P
Plan events	Keep options open
Like to make decisions	Like gathering information
Do tasks in order	Do several tasks randomly
More formal and conventional	More casual and unconventional
See things as black or white	See things in shades of gray

Want decisions made—may decide before all facts are in	Don't like final decisions—never have enough info—may even look for new options after decision is made
Like to be in control	Like adapting to new ideas
Strong work ethic: Work before play	Work AND play coexist
Responsible, firm, true to their word	Curious, adaptable, masters of improvising
May be unable to change	Flexible to making changes
Decisive, committed, determined	Enthusiastic, impetuous

How to communicate effectively with a J?

First of all, be on time.

They like for people to do what they say they are going to do.

Have your information organized and efficient.

They value efficiency, and when you have your information organized, they can determine that you value their time.

Design conversation so that you come to conclusions, and don't leave issues unresolved or open.

J's like things to be settled and decided. They are uncomfortable when things are left to chance. Having a lot of options open makes them feel out of control.

Allow them to make the decisions and organize the plans.

They like the control of knowing things are going to be organized to their liking.

25

Once the plans are made, stick with the plans!

> Do not try to change or make revisions. Changes are difficult for them.

If you are a helping professional dealing with a J during a crisis situation, help them to make a decision and plan about something quickly, based on sound information. Not big decisions during a crisis, but small decisions and plans that can bring a sense of stability to their lives.

Remember that J's do not like to change plans, so they will not react well to changes in those plans. They don't want to even consider new options when a decision has already been made. But, they also like to anticipate what they can ahead of time so that they can be prepared for it. When a plan does go badly and changes absolutely have to be made, a J will usually have an alternative plan already in mind.

How to communicate effectively with a "P"

Don't force them to make a decision right away.

> Leave options open with time for them to research and gather information. They are concerned that a decision will be made and then new information will be found that will change that decision. They want the option to change!

Provide several opportunities to discuss options and change plans.

> Delay a permanent decision until a later date. Make any plans easily adaptable to change. Again, as a P myself, I find that I often make the statement, "We'll just try this and see if it works. If it doesn't work, then we'll revise and go from there." I'm sure this must drive my J friends and co-workers crazy!

Give them lots of choices, and be open to new information and options yourself.

Again, personally I usually have a list of choices or options available for everything!

Approach them in an informal atmosphere.

They are casual and laid-back in their views and feel uncomfortable about formality.

Do not talk in terms of "either/or" choices

They understand things in shades of gray. It can be difficult to commit to such an extreme decision as "either this or that." They prefer choices with options.

If you are a helping professional dealing with a P personality during a crisis, help them to recognize their options and to get in touch with their ability to improvise. A P does not have alternative plans in place like the J does, but instead relies upon their own ability to be flexible and go with the flow. Helping them to look at the possibilities in their situation can be beneficial.

Section 3
SPs—Experiencers and Realists

This is the free-spirited group who live their lives out of their expressive natures and like to have options available to them. They are the "doers." They are interested in the "here and now" and are concerned with what works for them. They are the pleasure-seekers. They feel good about themselves when they are able to adjust themselves to the changing conditions in life. In fact, they are drawn to change and novelty like moths to a flame. They do well in crisis situations because they are able to adjust quickly and adapt themselves to rapidly changing circumstances.

The SP's are exciting, impulsive, and generous. They spend a lot of time looking for excitement and stimulation. They mainly notice things that are available to the senses—seeing, hearing, touching. They enjoy taking chances and being in risky situations; they may participate in activities like skydiving, rock climbing, or racecar driving. If it is there, if it is present, then they believe you should *do* something with it. Their entire self-perception is based on their ability to act boldly, confidently, and competitively; they will not be outdone. They believe that life is 100% for living—and they do it to their fullest ability. They love taking risks and, as you can already guess, are not impressed with "rules." They are not overly interested in long-term responsibility or commitments, either. They become bored rather quickly when the action isn't fast enough or when someone tries to restrict their freedom. They like to keep their relationships easygoing and free, without expectations or commitments.

Experiencers want to have fun, and they love sharing their fun with others. They are very willing to share whatever they have with their friends, families, and even acquaintances. In *The Pygmalion Project*, Stephen Montgomery describes half of the Experiencers (Cruise Ship and Raft) as "a large, friendly puppy gamboling and frisking its way through people's lives, offering unconditional and undiscriminating love, then moving on if threatened with collar and leash" (p. 18); the other half (Runabout and Kayak) are more manipulative. Stephen Montgomery says that they "feast on the give-and-take of politics and negotiations…" and that "they play to win." He describes them as "more of a fox than a puppy."

The Styles in this category are

ESTP: Runabout

ISTP: Kayak

ESFP: Cruise Ship

ISFP: Raft

ESTP Extroverted Sensing/Introverted Thinking

RUNABOUTS

The Runabouts theme is The Doer/Adventurer/Promoter. They love action and new experiences. Their driving force is their search for action, experience, and new challenges. They act first and rarely think of consequences. "Making things happen" seems to be their motto; getting people to have fun is their goal. They are flexible and resourceful, with an inherent zest for life. Their slogan could be "When all else fails, read the directions." They don't have time to stop and read the directions until something is not going the way they want.

I chose the Runabout—also known as the speedboat—to represent this style because the ESTP approaches life with enthusiasm and a sense of adventure. They experience life like kids in a candy store, fascinated and in eager anticipation of all of the good things they are about to encounter. The rush of ideas and the thrill of being spontaneous in their quest to do it all exhilarate them.

Runabouts are fast and exciting, and can be found in all expense brackets. These are the people that you see buzzing about from project to project, from place to place, with hardly time for a breath. I always wonder where they get their energy. Having worked with Attention Deficit Hyperactivity Disorder children, I wonder if a runabout is the natural mode of travel for these children. One of our puppies, Lucy, is also a natural runabout—she runs top speed from one exciting adventure to another. And when she stops running from place to place, then she goes in circles! She is a wonderful illustration of a true runabout.

Runabouts tend to be extremely witty, playful, and generous. They are very observant of the people around them and like to help others get what they want. They are very outgoing, spontaneous, unpredictable, action-oriented, clever, and generous. They don't always follow the rules and are rebellious toward structure and rigidity. In fact, if things become too routine, they will lose interest and become ready to move on to something else. They change their behavior easily to fit the situation. They are observant people and are aware of everything that goes on around them. Their governing characteristic is their animated approach to hands-on skills and real-life experiences. Commitment in relationships is an area that is difficult for them. They enjoy taking life as it comes, just doing whatever happens to be in their field of vision. They don't want to do anything that takes too long, because they are quickly up and running and ready to be on their way to the next adventure.

When approaching a runabout, keep in mind that they want things quick and exciting. They enjoy whatever comes along. They are adaptable and tolerant, but dislike long explanations—they have things to do and places to go. They are good to have around when you have a project that requires fast action and doesn't require a lot of effort spent in time-consuming details. An example would be news people—not the ones who do the research, but the reporter who is on the spot and breaking the story. They like to be able to see the immediate results of their work. Don't expect them to do a lot of reading or writing of reports. But do expect them to love mediation and negotiation and to be competitive. They love to win—to be top in their field.

I'm sure that we all have personal runabouts we have known. They wear us out with their energy and excitement. Four examples that immediately come to my mind are Robin Williams, Jim Carey, Eddie Murphy, and Madonna. They are all four among the most animated people I have ever seen. Just watching them wears me out! Life with them must surely be exciting and full of activity, as the description implies. Several articles referenced "James Bond" as also being a good representation of this type, because of his love of variety, excitement, and his high energy level. Robin Williams, Eddie Murphy, and Jim Carey are full of fast-paced comedy and action. Madonna's energy is directed toward her music and videos.

Below are quotes from or about these four personalities that represent their Runabout style:

Robin Williams:
"You're only given a little spark of madness. You mustn't lose it."
"Spring is nature's way of saying, 'Let's party!'"
"Ah...so many pedestrians, so little time..."
"Comedy is acting out optimism."
"After I quit drinking, I realized I am the same asshole I always was; I just have fewer dents in my car."

Jim Carey:
He has always aimed high, and at age ten, he sent his resume to Carol Burnett.
"My report card always said, 'Jim finishes first and then disrupts the other students'."
"What I have in common with the character in 'Truman' is this incredible need to please people. I feel like I want to take care of everyone, and I also feel this terrible guilt if I am unable to. And I have felt this way ever since all this success started."

"I really want to love somebody. I do. I just don't know if it's possible forever and ever."

"'You know what? I'm gonna do what I love to do, even if I starve to death doing it, you know, 'cause there's no safety.'"

On the making of *Ace Ventura*:
"*Ace Ventura* was not like the gift from God when I got it. It was like, okay, here's a story about a pet detective, and I liked [it], but [collaborator Steve Oedekerk and I] started [rewriting] from page one, night after night...Five hours of writing after we'd finished the *In Living Color* stuff, and well, okay, it was four hours of writing and an hour of putting our genitals on the Xerox machine. [It was] such a ridiculous thing that [I said] I'll write it, but I don't want to have to do it if [in the end]...I don't like it. [But] I just fell in love with it as I was doing it, because me and Steve just sat there and said, okay, what do people find it impossible to turn away from when it's on the news? Shark attack? Okay, let's put in a shark attack scene."

Eddie Murphy:
"I'd like to produce, direct, write, and star in a film in exactly the same way Chaplin did. I'll do that before I'm thirty."

Madonna:
"Better to live one year as a tiger than a hundred as a sheep."
"I have the same goal I've had ever since I was a girl. I want to rule the world."
"When I'm hungry, I eat. When I'm thirsty, I drink. When I feel like saying something, I say it."
"I'm tough, ambitious, and I know exactly what I want. If that makes me a bitch, okay."
"Sometimes you have to be a bitch to get things done."

"I am my own experiment. I am my own work of art."

"Listen, everyone is entitled to my opinion."

"I wouldn't have turned out the way I was if I didn't have all those old-fashioned values to rebel against."

"I stand for freedom of expression, doing what you believe in, and going after your dreams."

"I'd like to be more involved in making the world a better place."

"I am a survivor. I am like a cockroach—you just can't get rid of me."

"I think that everyone should get married at least once, so you can see what a silly, outdated institution it is."

"I'm anal-retentive. I'm a workaholic. I have insomnia. And I'm a control freak. That's why I'm not married. Who could stand me?"

"I miss New York. I still love how people talk to you on the street—just assault you and tell you what they think of your jacket."

"I've been popular and unpopular, successful and unsuccessful, loved and loathed, and I know how meaningless it all is. Therefore, I feel free to take whatever risks I want."

"We all play. I play, my husband, the nanny... My son uses all his adrenaline and then passes out. That's a good night."

"I stand for freedom of expression, doing what you believe in, and going after your dreams."

"Never forget to dream."

Another example is the rabbit in *Alice in Wonderland* who is always running around late and in a hurry. I find it amazing that the people who run around the fastest sometimes have no idea *where* they are going!

I have two friends, Lori and Jennifer, who are both examples of a Runabout personality. Lori and Jennifer are both extremely outgoing, love people, and enjoy being the center of attention. In fact, Lori worked with us for a time, but then moved on to a job that fit her personality better. During our hiring interviews, we immediately noticed Jennifer because she reminded us of Lori. Now we realize that we "picked up" on the same personality style that each of these Runabouts have. They both bring happiness and joy to the people around them. Their exuberant approach to life is evident in everything that they do: their speech—colorful and straightforward; their dress—casual, comfortable, and fun; their ease at being around people; their gaiety and openness. It's good to have a Runabout in the office to keep us filled with energy. Jennifer keeps us on our toes because we have to continuously explain the reason *why* she has to do something a certain way. So before we ask her to do something in a specific manner, we have to be sure *we* understand the reason why it has to be that way.

In the business world, you run across these boats in the sales personnel that you meet. I compare this type of Runabout to a fishing boat, because Runabouts can also be used as fishing boats. A salesman's goal is to catch you with his sales pitch. The professional salesperson wants to play with you on their line a little and then, when the timing is right, reel you in. The skills that would help them in a sales career would be their genuine love of people, their resourcefulness, their enthusiasm, their flexibility, and the fact that they are easygoing in their approach to life. If you have a runabout/fishing boat/salesman as a friend, they will enjoy helping you outsmart other fishing boats.

Other career possibilities are athletics, police work, paramedics, marketing, or negotiation—careers that require them to make quick moves or decisions.

Some of our best times are had with friends who are Runabouts. They are especially good to know when you want to have a fun and exciting weekend with lots of activity. They are very talkative and love to laugh and joke. They are your classic shoppers, always on the lookout for sales and bargains. But, personally, I'm always relieved to get back to homeport after a whirlwind outing with a Runabout. It requires a lot of energy to keep pace with them—but then, I'm an Introvert.

If you are in a relationship with a Runabout, it will be exciting, fun, and full of activity. If you have lots of energy and like to be active, they can create an exciting life for you. Commitment is not a strong point for the Runabout. So if you are married to a Runabout and are not a Runabout yourself, you will want to make sure that your partner has lots of exciting activities to keep them occupied. If you are smart and in a relationship with a Runabout that is also a fishing boat, you will let the fishing boat catch you, not the other way around. Remember, it is all about the challenge. After he/she has caught you, they will keep you as a trophy to show off to others. Don't be insulted by this, because a fishing boat treasures their prize catch completely and will treat you like a valuable gem (or stuffed fish, whatever the case may be). There will be a story about how they caught you to tell over and over again to your grandchildren. Once he/she has the relationship in order, they will turn their attention to the challenge of catching whatever is in their business world or hobby area.

A Runabout/fishing boat will continue to change the lure until it gets what it wants. In a relationship, that might be attention, favors, presents, guilt, anger, worry, or fear. A Runabout/fishing boat loves the challenge of catching something, so it will keep throwing out bait as long as you play the game. That is called "working" the fish. In this case, *you* are the fish. When a Runabout/fishing boat discovers the lure that works with you, they will continue to use it. Therefore, be careful which lure you are susceptible to. If it is guilt, then the Runabout/fishing boat will become a master of bringing out the guilt in you. If it is anger, then they can become pros at inducing anger. Again, they are very keen at picking up on subtle nuances through their keen observational abilities, so be careful what you react to. This is another area where it is an extreme advantage to know yourself and to like who you are as a person. Then what will "hook" you is sincerity, acceptance, and love. They can also become pros at continuing to hook you with their sincerity, generousness, and down-to-earth love of life.

Barnum and Bailey come to mind here. They're known as the "greatest show on earth"—and also were very successful in knowing how to attract people to that show. They were extremely adept at throwing out bait to reel us, the public, in to their show. But I, for one, enjoyed being reeled in to their show.

What a Runabout needs from others:

- Respect the Runabout's need for freedom.

- Be direct, concise, and unemotional when talking about issues.

- Enjoy their fun-loving and highly social nature.

- Join in and have fun in some of the adventures they have.

- Keep it simple.

- Give them several options to choose from.

If you have a Runabout in your life and you notice that they seem moody, unenergetic, hypersensitive, or compulsive, or that they are starting to withdrawal from their usual activities, this is a sign they are overwhelmed with something in their lives. You can help the Runabout by sitting down with them and helping them to reassess their situation, and to look at it differently.

If you are a Runabout/fishing boat and experiencing some problems because of your personality style, here are some suggestions that might benefit you:

- Learn how to recognize feelings and not just be busy with external activities. Believe it or not, meditation can help. But for you, short meditations. There is a book, *The Eight Minute Meditation*, which may be appropriate for you.

- Realize that each person you allow into your life is different, with his or her own values, communication styles, and needs.

- You may find that the overwhelmed feeling you are experiencing is not the need for another challenge, but a natural response to a steady diet of constant activities. It may very well be time to reflect about what you can bring to your life, finding purpose. Learn the ability to stick with the things you choose.

- The word "boring" can be a big warning sign for you. Whenever you are starting to feel bored with life, stop. Look at what it is that you are avoiding.

- Imagine the worst things that could happen, and allow yourself to actually sit down and come up with plans that would address these things.

- Stop and look at your negative feelings. Allowing yourself to experience your negative feelings as well as your joy will enhance your life. Start by simply recognizing and accepting that you do experience negative feelings. Learn to identify them.

Exercises that can help you:

Notice how thinking about what you are going to do next can keep you from enjoying the present. Next time you become bored, *stop.* Ask yourself what it feels like. What thoughts are going on about it?

During times of extreme stress, crisis, or grief, a Roundabout will tend to become outward-focused and want to run around taking care of everyone else. This can help them get through the initial shock and reaction to the situation. But then they need to be able to take the time to slow down and look inside themselves and take care of themselves too.

In the area of spirituality, Runabouts prefer connecting with God while they are outside enjoying nature and doing real-life activities with other people. Churches which have group activities like biking, sports teams, or hiking would appeal to this group. They prefer to experience hands-on activities that they can directly apply to their lives. When connected to their spirituality, they can see the spiritual, the Divine, in the ordinary material world. It is a feeling of wonder and awe at the beauty of life that really personifies a Roundabout.

"I am thankful for

My love of this life
My realistic grasp of situations
My resourcefulness and quick responsiveness
The way I can catch the joys of the moment

In the storms of life, I can find shelter by

Making time to pause and reflect
Envisioning the future with positive expectations
Assessing my true priorities

To honor myself and my pathway to God, I can

Search for ways to integrate soul work and the activities I enjoy
Search the company of others who find spirituality in the midst of life
Retreat, if only rarely, to give my spiritual side the attention it needs" *Soul Types*, page 58

ESTP Prayer: God, help me slow downandnotrushthrougheveryth ingIdo.

ISTP   Introverted Thinking /Extroverted Sensing

KAYAK

The theme of a Kayak is Crafter/Operator. They thrive on challenges and love to have the freedom for discovering their own clever solutions. Their theme is their action-driven orientation. Their driving force is their need to understand how the things in their life work. These people tend to be private and like to be alone. They can seem to others as cool or reserved. They are sometimes described as aloof. Their motto would be, "Live and let live."

I chose a Kayak to represent the Crafter/Operator because a Kayak is a solitary mode of transportation that is capable of taking a person into remote adventures. A Kayak is a boat for a loner who has individualistic, high-risk pursuits. Kayaks like to go where other boats cannot go. They love to solve problems, and when they are not in the process of solving a specific problem, they tend to become quiet and analytical observers of what is going on around them.

These people feel most alive when they are doing something independent and risky. They live for the moment, are action-oriented, and take risks. They have an inexhaustible curiosity toward the world around them. The do not like to follow rules or authority. They are also adept at using tools and instruments, and at noticing variations and patterns in the things around them. They love to figure things out on their own, and sometimes are even accused of "living in a world of their own."

A Kayak is a self-contained, isolated type of individual. They are very much into remote, individualistic pursuits. You won't know many kayaks for this reason. They very much follow their own inner guidance away from other people. They prefer to spend their lives in secluded areas, exploring and learning about subjects of which the rest of us never even dream. These people reach inside themselves to that hidden and spiritual world that capitalizes on their imagination. They can live lives of excitement and challenge when crashing through the surge of white waters never experienced before, or they can live a life of quiet and peaceful meditation. Their lives are within themselves.

A Kayak is not a social mode of traveling through life; they much prefer physical, individualistic pursuits. They can be extremely addicted to adrenaline-producing activities, and they love being in the moment. They prefer to work with objects and things rather than with people, although they do have a playful and spontaneous side when you get to know them well.

An example of a Kayak personality is Robert Redford, who likes to live his life in seclusion. Other examples would be Charles Bronson, James Dean, Frank Zappa, Woody Allen, and Amelia Earhart.

> **Robert Redford**: "I mean, I used to race cars when I was a kid, so it's very hard for me to let go of the idea of a racing vehicle in my life… but for me, those days have pretty much ended, and now I really do spend pretty much of my time on horseback. And I'm very happy because of it. I smell and see and feel things I never would have dreamed to feel if I were swishing

through on a car. So that is not a loss for me; it's actually a wonderful gain."

"I started out in life to be an artist, a painter. I see the world through that lens, all my life. It caught me by surprise the first time I directed, and I suddenly was putting that to use—that sense of spatial formation and control within a frame. I had thought that part of my life was behind me, but it wasn't. And I was so happy to rediscover it—it's one of the real joys of directing, but I have very strong feelings about the visual elements of film."

Sport is a wonderful metaphor for life. Of all the sports that I played—skiing, baseball, fishing—there is no greater example than golf, because you're playing against yourself and nature.

"We do not own this place, we are just passengers."

Charles Bronson: "He was a very quiet and introspective collaborator, often sitting in a corner for much of a shoot, and listening to a director's instructions, not saying a word until the cameras started rolling."

When responding to critics' complaints, he said: "We don't make movies for critics, since they don't pay to see them anyhow."

James Dean: "James Dean was little more than a boy when he died, killed at twenty-four on the highway near Paso Robles, California, on September 30, 1955, while on his way to a sports car meet. But even during his short life, Dean was widely known as a nonconformist—a rebel who had taken Hollywood by storm and who did as he pleased. Dean's recklessness and commitment to having lived his life to the fullest had its appeal as well."

Rebel For All Seasons
By Ron Martinetti

"A neurotic person has the necessity to express himself, and my neuroticism manifests itself in the dramatic..." He was-cool; the perfect quote was always on his lips.
"Dream as if you'll live forever. Live as if you'll die today."
"Only the gentle are ever really strong.'
"I know, Mike, we all march to a different drumbeat."

Frank Zappa: "It has never mattered to me that thirty million people might think I'm wrong. The number of people who thought Hitler was right did not make him right..."
"Why do you necessarily have to be wrong just because a few million people think you are?"
"I never set out to be weird. It was always the other people who called me weird"
(Frank Zappa, to Baltimore Sun, Oct. 12, 1986).

"Frank Zappa was the father of invention, the most caustic iconoclast of the rock-and-roll era. 'My job,' he once said, 'is extrapolating everything to its most absurd extreme.'
"Blessed with an agile mind that embraced astoundingly diverse styles of music and rejected moral and intellectual hypocrisy, Zappa made non-conformity his credo. Experimentalism was his methodology, satire and social commentary his weapons, and the American way of life his target."
"His own name came to stand for restless invention and reinvention. Zappa was a pioneer in digital recording technology and a textbook study in the search for artistic independence."
Hot Shot Digital Web Page Rock Tributes

Woody Allen:

"As the poet said, 'Only God can make a tree' -- probably because it's so hard to figure out how to get the bark on."

"The good people sleep much better at night than the bad people. Of course, the bad people enjoy the waking hours much more."

"His films have linked the borders of drama and comedy, while continually being entertaining and honest. A very quiet man, Woody frequently declines the offer to make an appearance to promote his upcoming films. Details to his films are also kept relatively quiet, the trailers viewed in the theaters usually being the only information the viewer will see before the movie is released into the theaters. Although this is the case, most Woody Allen films are well worth the wait, time and money."

Amelia Earhart:

"Adventure is worthwhile in itself."

"Courage is the price that life exacts for granting peace.

Never do things others can do and will do if there are things others cannot do or will not do."

"Flying may not be all plain sailing, but the fun of it is worth the price."

"As soon as we left the ground, I knew I myself had to fly!"

"Never interrupt someone doing what you said couldn't be done."

"The most difficult thing is the decision to act, the rest is merely tenacity. The fears are paper tigers. You can do anything you decide to do. You can act to change and control your life; and the procedure, the process is its own reward."

"The most effective way to do it, is to do it."

"After midnight the moon set and I was alone with the stars. I have often said that the lure of flying is the lure of beauty, and I need no other flight to convince me that the reason flyers fly, whether they know it or not, is the esthetic appeal of flying."

"Anticipation, I suppose, sometimes exceeds realization."

"Not much more than a month ago I was on the other shore of the Pacific, looking westward. This evening, I looked eastward over the Pacific. In those fast-moving days which have intervened, the whole width of the world has passed behind us—except this broad ocean. I shall be glad when we have the hazards of its navigation behind us."

-- Amelia Earhart, several days before she left for Howland Island and disappeared

"...decide...whether or not the goal is worth the risks involved. If it is, stop worrying...."

"I lay no claim to advancing scientific data other than advancing flying knowledge. I can only say that I do it because I want to."

"Worry retards reaction and makes clear-cut decisions impossible."

"The stars seemed near enough to touch and never before have I seen so many. I always believed the lure of flying is the lure of beauty, but I was sure of it that night."

"My ambition is to have this wonderful gift produce practical results for the future of commercial flying and for the women who may want to fly tomorrow's planes."

"Preparation, I have often said, is rightly two-thirds of any venture."

"The woman who can create her own job is the woman who will win fame and fortune."

"It is far easier to start something than it is to finish it."

"Courage is the price that Life exacts for granting peace, The soul that knows it not, knows no release from little things."

"The soul's dominion? Each time we make a choice, we pay with courage to behold restless day and count it fair."

"Women must try to do things as men have tried. When they fail, their failure must be but a challenge to others."

"[Women] must pay for everything.... They do get more glory than men for comparable feats. But, also, women get more notoriety when they crash."

"...now and then women should do for themselves what men have already done—occasionally what men have not done—thereby establishing themselves as persons, and perhaps encouraging other women toward greater independence of thought and action. Some such consideration was a contributing reason for my wanting to do what I so much wanted to do."

"Adventure is worthwhile in itself."

"Never do things others can do and will do, if there are things others cannot do or will not do."

Quotes **about** Amelia Earhart

"Being men and being engaged in a highly essential phase of the serious business of air transportation, they [airline mechanics] all naturally had preconceived notions about a woman pilot bent on a 'stunt' flight— not very favorable notions either. It was, undoubtedly, something of a shock to discover that the 'gal' with whom they had to deal not only was an exceptionally pleasant human being who 'knew her stuff,' but that she knew exactly what she wanted done, and had sense

enough to let them alone while they did it. There was
an almost audible clatter of chips falling off skeptical
masculine shoulders."
—C.B. Allen, New York Herald Tribune

"Amelia is a grand person for such a trip. She is the
only woman flyer I would care to make such an
expedition with. Because in addition to being a fine
companion and pilot, she can take hardship as well as
a man—and work like one."
—Fred Noonan, Amelia's navigator for the around-
the-world flight

"Amelia Earhart came perhaps before her time...the
smiling, confident, capable, yet compassionate human
being is one of which we can all be proud."
-- Walter J. Boyne

The only Kayak I am aware of that I have known is Tim, and I have
to admit, I didn't know him very well. Tim kept to himself, and did
what Kayaks do—he found his own adventures. He was very gentle
and shy. No one realized it at the time, but he did not like rules. He
didn't cut his grass because he didn't want to kill anything that was
living. Then one day Tim just packed up and moved. No one knew
where he went, and no one has heard from him since. His brother
just says that he is doing well and doing his own thing.

In a career, Kayaks tend to gravitate toward professions that have lots
of variety and action and do not have a lot of structure. Examples
of these high-variety professions would be policemen, pilots,
athletes, entrepreneurs, and forensic pathologists. All of these would
incorporate the interests and abilities of the Kayak. They would
each use the skills of variety, action, trouble-shooting, risk-taking,
independence, flexibility, and determination. They are the people you
work with who are difficult to get to know, who do their own thing,
in their own way. They will do their best in situations where they
need to react "on the fly," so to speak. They don't like the planning
and discussion stages; they just want to *do*. They like to work *things*

instead of people. They may also gravitate toward careers such as engineering or designing equipment. Computers are a natural fit for these inquisitive loners. And they love information and facts.

If you are in a relationship with a Kayak it will take a lot of patience on your part, because Kayaks tend to take the relationship "one day at a time". They are not very feeling-oriented and do not readily show their emotions. They are interested in action and new experiences, so commitment is not one of the things that come naturally to them. If you can remember that they are fiercely independent, do not like being controlled, and definitely need room to go their own way, then you may have a chance with them. You will have to remember they value their freedom—not to roam to other ports, but to just live their lives in their own way and as the impulse strikes them. Don't take it personally if they are ready to take off into a new and exciting adventure and haven't discussed it with you. They are extremely solitary and independent, and they tend to just take each day on a moment-by-moment basis. They do appreciate beauty and are very connected to their five senses, and so will often be very sensual in the bedroom.

They are fun, playful, and adventurous and will share some of their adventures with you if you don't try to restrict them or place demands on them. Don't try to plan or schedule events for them; remember, they want to act on the impulse of the moment—to fly, soar, run, and rappel into life as the mood strikes them.

What a Kayak needs from you:

- Give them lots of space and freedom to follow their impulses and explore their world.

- Don't try to control them.

- Be patient.

- Do not use emotional appeals, and do not force them to share themselves with you.

- Most of all, don't pressure them to tell you how they feel.

If there is a Kayak in your life and they are becoming overwhelmed, you will notice that they are beginning to become obstinate or overreacting to your suggestions. You can help them by asking them to join you in some other kind of activity, or maybe asking them to do something for you. Getting their minds on something else can give them time to refocus and regroup.

If you are a Kayak and having problems because of your personality style, here are some suggestions that may help you:

- Learn to open yourself up to experiences that are outside of your comfort zone.

- Allow yourself to discuss and reassess your ideas and thoughts with others, even though it does not come easily for you.

- Be around people who love to be active with you.

- Learn to accept the principles of others around you who do follow the social rules and guidelines.

- Learn to begin to recognize your feelings.

- Learn to be more personal with people, commenting on the things you like about them instead of just the things you don't like.

- Find joy in everyday occurrences.

Exercise that may be helpful to you:

Keep a journal about the feeling(s) you have when you have the urge to isolate. When you need to get away from everyone, what are your thoughts? What are your feelings? Are there certain situations that cause you to isolate and withdraw more than others?

The next time you feel driven to participate in a risk-taking activity or pursuit, notice your thoughts at the time. What are you saying to yourself about the activity? How do you feel?

During extreme stress, crisis, or grief a Kayak will usually take off on its own to go inside and process the experience on its own. Once the processing time is over, they need to come back to others and connect to the people in their lives. But they need to be allowed to connect in a way that is comfortable for them, and not be pressured into activities and situations which would place more stress upon them. Give them the space they need, but be ready to take wordless hikes with them when they are ready.

Kayaks tend to recognize the spiritual in everyday activities rather than to actively seek out a place of worship. They prefer to do things that they can see are a benefit to others; they need to see the purpose of what they are doing. As they grow spiritually, they will begin to feel a connection with everything around them. This feeling of connection may begin with nature, to notice how each plant affects the others. Over time, this awareness of connections between things spreads to their relationships with others.

"I am thankful for

My efficiency and ability to get things done
My quiet commitment to lending a hand when needed
My reasoning, which defines what is
The practical bent I provide in using systems and information

In the storms of life, I can find shelter by

Reserving time for reflection and analysis
Finding ways to acknowledge and deal with my emotions
Reassessing reality, reviewing what can and cannot change

To honor myself and my pathway to God, I can

Satisfy my logic and my rational side as I determine my needs for soulwork

Reconsider what I value, the relationships and purposes that will make my life most meaningful

Acknowledge the spiritual in my experience—finding the consistencies and truths that are manifestations of God"

Soul Types, page 218

ISTP Prayer: God, help me to consider other people's feelings, even if most of them *are* overly sensitive.

ESFP   Extroverted Sensing/Introverted Feeling

CRUISE SHIP

The theme of a Cruse ship is Joker/Performer. They thrive on social interaction and entertaining. Their drive is the challenge of the unknown, and their goal is to make a difference. They are exuberant in their approach to life, fun-loving, playful, and spontaneous. Their driving force is their excitement toward involvement with new activities and people, especially helping types of endeavors. Their motto could very easily be, "You only go around once in life..." and they like to create an atmosphere of "Come on everybody, lets party!"

I used a Cruise Ship to represent this style because my son is a Cruise Ship and said that this is the kind of boat that would represent him. Cruise Ships like lots of people around them all of the time, and they believe in having fun. Friends and family are the most important things in their lives, and they make it their job to make sure that everyone has a good time. One of their skills is bringing various factions of people together.

You'll always be able to recognize a cruise ship; they are the ones who want to party and travel with large groups of people wherever they go. They are *never* alone if they have anything to do with it. They are a party waiting to happen. They are friendly, approachable, energetic, talkative, and spontaneous. In fact, they love the telephone and will have one nearby at all times. They will also be observant in making sure that others are enjoying themselves, and will readily pick up on problems in other people. They will share whatever they have with you without a second thought. They are always ready to help others with their warm and practical actions of assistance. They are true and genuine people persons, and they dislike being alone. There are always people coming and going wherever they are; sometimes it feels like a three-ring circus to other people around them.

Cruise Ships enjoy living in the moment and can be very focused and persistent—when they are doing something they want to be doing. When they need to do something that they don't want to do, then they can have a difficult time staying on task. Their challenge is to direct their abilities into areas that can bring about accomplishment and creative goals; otherwise they become a Cruise Ship sailing around with no particular port in mind.

They are extremely talented at speaking and are very resourceful at wordplay and stories. They tend to skip around from topic to topic and wherever the next impulse takes them. It is sometimes a challenge to the other personality styles to follow their conversations. When they write, their style is an appealing, conversationalist style that is loaded with pertinent facts and details. They are especially creative when writing about people, and they will often use lots of anecdotes and true stories about their subjects.

Elvis Presley would illustrate a Cruise Ship personality, at least as much as that life was forced upon him. Elvis wanted large groups of people to be with him all the time. He kept a group of friends nearby every minute of the day. He was ready to travel at a moment's notice—even if only for his favorite peanut butter sandwich. He was extremely playful and fun-loving. His fame caused him to deteriorate from his preferred way of being.

"A live concert to me is exciting because of all the electricity that is generated in the crowd and onstage. It's my favorite part of the business—live concerts."
"Ah just act the way ah feel."
"Music should be something that makes you gotta move, inside or outside."

Other examples would be Ronald Reagan, Magic Johnson, and Goldie Hawn.

Ronald Reagan: Reagan possessed a truly amazing gift to communicate with people. He was even called "The Great Communicator."
"Ronald Reagan was a big-picture person. I don't think he was a detail person," said Bonser, also director of IU's Arts Administration Program. "He was criticized sometimes for maybe not being as up on the details as he might be."
Hershey added that Reagan's positive personality and ability to effectively communicate his messages helped him move the party in a new direction. "Part of it was the way Reagan said things, and part of it was the kind of person he was," she said. "He had a sunny personality…."
"With simple messages and a quick wit that deflected his shortcomings and produced across-the-board chuckles, Reagan made Americans feel better about themselves and their nation. That counted for a lot."
"The leader of the free world gave the impression that he was as happy on horseback at his beloved California Rancho del Cielo as he was at the White House. He kept jellybeans on his Oval Office desk, and he told jokes everybody would get—often to his political advantage."

Reagan Quotes:

"Going to college offered me the chance to play football for four more years."

"How can a president not be an actor?"

"I am not worried about the deficit. It is big enough to take care of itself."

"It's silly talking about how many years we will have to spend in the jungles of Vietnam when we could pave the whole country and put parking stripes on it and still be home by Christmas."

"It's true hard work never killed anybody, but I figure, why take the chance?"

"Life is one grand, sweet song, so start the music."

"Peace is not the absence of conflict—it is the ability to handle conflict by peaceful means."

"Politics is just like show business. You have a hell of an opening, coast for a while, and then have a hell of a close."

"Politics is not a bad profession. If you succeed, there are many rewards; if you disgrace yourself, you can always write a book."

"Recession is when a neighbor loses his job. Depression is when you lose yours."

"The problem is not that people are taxed too little—the problem is that government spends too much."

"Today, if you invent a better mousetrap, the government comes along with a better mouse."

"We can't help everyone, but everyone can help someone."

"You can tell a lot about a fellow's character by his way of eating jellybeans."

Magic Johnson:
Stars of Today
Legends of yesterday

Earvin "Magic" Johnson is an impressive man. He lights up the room with his smile, and people gravitate toward his dynamic personality.

Those who have followed his accomplishments have seen that this man has a purpose in life, a legacy, and an enthusiasm for living to share with those around him.

The Johnson philosophy is that all business ventures must have a redeeming social value.

Beyond his charisma, popular appeal, and high visibility worldwide is a man dedicated to making society a better place for all to live.

National Sports Agency
NBA@NationalSportsAgency.com

"Magic Johnson Theatres are the result of a shared passion for filmed entertainment and community development. 'Building Magic Johnson Theatres has been a dream realized,' said Mr. Johnson. 'This has been a perfect vehicle for me to actively participate in providing quality family entertainment to those neighborhoods that have been underserved.'"

"That first game, I was so excited and so nervous that I ran out of the court leading my team out. I'm trying to be cool but not show that I'm so excited. By the time I get down there, I'm about to lay it up—the first layup, I trip and stumble and started rolling. That's how nervous I was. I turned around and they were just dying laughing at me."

"All kids need is a little help, a little hope, and somebody who believes in them."

"Ask not what your teammates can do for you. Ask what you can do for your teammates."

"You're the only one who can make the difference. Whatever your dream is, go for it."

Goldie Hawn: "At 58, Goldie Hawn still holds the zest of a twenty-year-old. Her laughter is contagious and her free spirit draws you to her."
"Hawn has described herself as having a 'light personality and a deep-thinking brain,' and she enjoys getting wild and feeling free."
"Goldie is a firm believer in laughter as the best medicine to heal anxiety and depression, and she's on a personal mission to teach others how to be happier. An eternal optimist, she awakes each morning looking forward to the day ahead, and claims meditation and yoga as the key to her youthful, carefree attitude."
"She hasn't changed all that much in that regard, as in 2001, the *L.A. Times* referred to Goldie as 'the ultimate good-time gal: fun, free and non-threatening to men.'"

"I'll have a lot of wrinkles on my face, but I feel like my heart will be fat and full."
Goldie Hawn

As I said earlier, my son Joshua is also a Cruise Ship personality. This is difficult for his father, the Aircraft Carrier, to understand sometimes. Josh loves being with people. He was a "people" person from the time he was a baby. No matter where we go, he finds and makes friends. He is happy, fun-loving, and out-going. And need I mention talkative? When he was nine years old, I had a friend pick him up and take him home for me. The friend said that Josh talked nonstop from the moment he got in the car until they reached my house, which was fifteen miles away. Josh has many out-going activities: he likes rock-climbing, playing frisbee, hiking, biking, cooking—all with and for friends, of course. He likes to keep his options open and has a problem with trying to schedule too many activities and people into his life; he wants to do it all!

Josh does take criticism extremely personally; he wants so much to make everyone happy. He loves and takes great care to help people whenever he can. He is also an Eagle Scout.

Josh had a very serious auto accident a few years ago, and the hospital personnel were amazed at the number of friends that Josh had who visited him; the information desk attendant even came up to his room to meet "the kid that had so many friends". When he was able to come home, my house was constantly full of his friends and visitors. It truly was a three-ring-circus atmosphere. His friends are what pulled him through his injuries. I truly believe that if not for his friends, he would not have healed so completely.

You'll find Cruise Ships working in jobs where they are around large numbers of people. They will be the ones who make plans for celebrations for everyone. They will organize all the office parties, birthdays, anniversaries, holidays, etc. They are the socializers, the team players. They need to be in a profession where they have a lot of contact with people. They love children and animals, dislike structure and routine, and are independent, resourceful and spontaneous. They need to stay away from career choices which are filled with details and isolation. Good career choices would be actor/actress, sales representative, photographer, counselor, public relations, childcare, teaching, radio, or event coordinator.

Having a Cruise Ship friend is wonderful. You know a party will always be in progress. And if for some reason there is not one at the moment, all you have to do is mention it, and it's assured there will soon be one. They are genuinely interested in and caring toward other people. They get sincere enjoyment from everything they experience in life, and they love bringing as many people along with them as they can. Don't expect a lot of individual, one-on-one time with them, because they attract a lot of friends and are extremely popular. They are usually breathlessly rushing from one activity to the next. They are quick to be of assistance to their friends, and they love to hear that their assistance was appreciated and made a difference.

If you are married to a Cruise Ship, you'll know it because you will attend, and host, more parties than you ever imagined. Hopefully you like to travel in large groups as much as your partner, or you'll be in for some discouraging times. A cruise ship will keep your life full of people, places, and excitement. Sometimes it may be difficult to keep the basics done.

Since Cruise Ships like to live in the moment, commitment is a sticky point for them. They love making their partner happy, but don't want to think about the future. Their goal is to be happy and to make the other people in their lives happy. So if you can wait around long enough to get that commitment, you will have to show that you can "go with the flow" in their spur-of-the-moment lifestyles.

What a Cruise Ship needs from you:

- Have fun with them.

- Appreciate their enthusiasm.

- Don't try to restrict their freedom.

- Learn to enjoy their spontaneity—be flexible.

- Accept the enormous amounts of friends and people that they have in their life.

- Let them know you appreciate the many ways they will show my affection for you.

It is usually easy to spot when a Cruise Ship is feeling overwhelmed. They will develop a very uncharacteristic negative perspective, their priorities will become unbalanced, and they will become depressed and withdrawn.

To help them during these times, you can

- Help them to talk about what is bothering them.

- Encourage them to slow down and take time to look inside themselves to learn some new perspectives.

- Respect their privacy.

- Let them know how much you appreciate them.

- Remind them of all the friends they have who care about them.

- Ask them to cheer you up.

If you are a Cruise Ship and you notice you are not up for your usual form of entertainment, some things you can consider:

- Reduce the amount of your activities and take time to process your feelings.

- Look realistically at the future possibilities of the situation.

- Spend some time in solitude.

- Talk to someone you trust about what is going on with you.

- Don't always expect the worst when something goes wrong. Look at the positives that can happen also— open yourself to looking at things in broader and more imaginative terms.

- Look at your boundaries. Are you letting others overstep their bounds?

Exercise that may be helpful:

Learn to listen to your body. Are you getting enough rest? Are you eating properly? Ask yourself what *you* need.

For a couple of days, make a list of all of your activities, and things you do for your friends. Are there some things you can do less frequently? Are you giving yourself time to be spontaneous? Give yourself a little "breathing room" to be able to just be the exuberant person that you are.

When there is severe stress, crisis, or grief in the life of a Cruise Ship, they will definitely need the support of their friends. But they also need some alone time to be able to get in touch with their feelings about the stressful situation. Friends are their support, but when friends are constantly present, it tends to keep the Cruise Ship focused outside of themselves and does not allow them the opportunity to get in touch with the feelings connected to the situation. Again, I can use the example of my son, Joshua. After his accident, it was the continuous presence of his friends that helped him through the recovery period, because their presence helped keep him focused outwardly and not dwell on his injuries. But there came a time, when he was in a physically stronger condition, that he needed to be alone in order to look inside and process the accident and the effects it had on him. Spiritual practice for a Cruise Ship usually focuses on connections with other people. Many Cruise Ships find a real closeness to God when they are out in nature with people they feel close to. My son, Josh, is not only a Cruise Ship but also an Eagle Scout. Adventure outings with other Scouts have brought him a real sense of closeness and connection to God. As a Cruise Ship matures in their spirituality, they develop the ability to notice the love that is all around them in everything and everyone they see; they begin to be aware that they are a connecting part of that love.

"I am thankful for

My enjoyment of each new day and the fresh wonders it brings
The varied ways I offer practical help to others
The enthusiasm I add to each endeavor and to those around me
My openness to exploring, experimenting, and experiencing spirituality in different ways

In the storms of life, I can find shelter by

Seeking support from those who know me well
Reserving some time so that I'll have renewed energy for myself as well as for others
Focusing on the unseen, those inexplicable aspects of our lives

To honor myself and my pathway to God, I can

See God in the here and now by experiencing the Creator in all of creation
Connect with others to join in celebrating our spiritual journeys
Become comfortable with listening to my dreams and hopes for the future" *Soul Types*, page 13

ESFP Prayer: God, help me take life more seriously, especially parties and dancing!

ISFP Introverted Sensing/Extroverted Feeling

RAFT

A Raft's theme is Childlike/Composer/Sensualist. They are naturally spontaneous and live very much in the "now." They focus on each experience in order to become harmonious with that experience. They thrive on the freedom to vary what they do. They love their leisure time, and will look for many ways to relax and play. Their driving force is their deep-felt caring for living things and their spontaneous playfulness. Their motto is "stop and smell the roses." Their theme is diversity and sensation.

I chose a Raft to represent the Childlike/Sensualist because they have very little interest in controlling others and are very willing to follow along in order to please their friends. A Raft is free and unencumbered with which direction it is going. An example would be a person of this style who enjoys beach-combing, hiking, exploring nature, or just spending time with animals with no particular goal in mind. They love time spent where they don't have to focus on a specific outcome. They are very flexible in their outlook, plans, and day-to-day living. They are very open-minded, tolerant, and unbiased in their approach to life. They are seen as being "free spirits."

They are easily distracted, sensitive, gentle, and easy-going. They find great beauty and joy in simple pleasures. They prize freedom and have a great attraction to nature. If an animal is being abused, they can rush in "where angels fear to tread." They are oblivious to the danger to themselves. Rafts have a special connection with children and animals, and they may even carry this affinity over into the area of plants and herbs. In fact, they have such a close connection and empathy that they may make animals, children, or plants a "mission" in their lives.

Rafts are the people who drift along through life, going wherever the currents take them. They are not interested in leading or controlling the other people in their lives and, in fact, are more concerned with observing, sensing, and experiencing their own little piece of the water. You can usually recognize a raft when you meet one by his lack of a sense of direction. Some will seem carefree, and others will seem a bit bewildered. You've heard the saying, "He is a child, teach him." Well, this is a child and he needs to be taught. This can be an easy, relaxing lifestyle, or it can be a disaster. The difference lies in the type of currents where they find themselves navigating.

Their speaking pattern is geared toward what they are able to physically sense. They prefer to express themselves through action rather than words. They choose things that can be touched, seen, or felt, not the world of inner contemplation and ideas. Their senses are extremely well-developed, and they find great appreciation in beauty of all kinds. For this reason, many Rafts are drawn to artistic pursuits such as dancing, painting, drawing, writing, etc.

In romance, a Raft wants it to be "fun." Their partner will need to provide unending varieties of unexpected emotional and physical stimulation. They like lots of sensual diversity and spontaneity. Indeed, they are the true "sensualist" of the personality styles.

I can't help but think of Pauly Shore when I think of a Raft, at least the way he presents himself in public. (He may be a submarine underneath!) He just seems to drift along through life wherever the currents take him, with no obvious direction in mind. He appears to be in the here and now, with no thought of the future to mar his progress. I, being a true caretaker, always want to take him by the hand and lead him to firmer ground.

Critic Quote: "Maybe the point of the Pauly Shore character is that he's cool and unengaged most of the time. Bombs explode all around him, but he's laid-back and doesn't let anything get to him. Instead of laughs, we get to see him having a good time."

TIMELINE
written by Justin
http://www.mutantreviewers.com/rtimepauly.html

The Rise and Fall of Mr. Pauly Shore

Is there a part in there for me? Hey, is there a part in there for me?

The female version of the Pauly Shore characters would be Phoebe on *Friends,* the television sitcom. Can you see the resemblances? Imagine a show with both Phoebe and Pauly Shore in it!

Phoebe: [Right after playing a song in the coffee shop] "If you want to receive e-mails about my upcoming shows, then please give me money so I can buy a computer."
Phoebe: "Observe the art of seduction. Watch, learn, and don't eat my cookie."
Phoebe: "I may play the fool at times, but I'm a little more than just a pretty blonde girl with an ass that won't quit."

In the literature, other examples of Rafts are Brigitte Bardot, Paul McCartney, Doris Day, Liberace, Elizabeth Taylor, Marilyn Monroe, and Cher.

Brigitte Bardot:

Bardot retired from acting in 1974 but still makes headlines today with her many animal-rights causes.

Desperately Seeking Saison: A Love Potion to Savour

by Rich Rabassa and Ale Clayson

She will make it after the movie of Nina Companeez, and decide to dedicate herself to the reason of animals.

Already in 1962, she was the first, in France, to denounce the barbaric methods of slaughtering butcher shop animals publicly. She'll get of the Public Powers the obligation to use a previous blackout material to slaughtering. Henceforth free of all film engagement, she gives all her energy to animal protection. It was she who, in 1977, denounced the atrocious massacre of baby seals, and she'll fight until she gets a ban on the trade of their fur.

In 1986, Brigitte Bardot created her Foundation to Saint Tropez Foundation, and in June 1987, she auctioned many objects, pieces of jewelry, and personal effects to get the 3 million francs required by the French legislature. In December 1991, she even parted with her legendary property *The Madrague* to increase the capital and to get the recognition of the state.

Membre de ClickFR, Reseau francophone
Paie-Par-Click Geocities

Brigitte quotes:

"A photograph can be an instant of life captured for eternity that will never cease looking back at you."

"It is better to be unfaithful than to be faithful without wanting to be."

"I gave my beauty and my youth to men. I am going to give my wisdom and experience to animals."

"It is sad to grow old, but nice to ripen."

"I don't think when I make love."
"Men are beasts, and even beasts don't behave as they do."

Paul McCartney:
"In the end, the love you take is equal to the love you make."
"If slaughterhouses had glass walls, everyone would be a vegetarian."
"I used to think anyone doing anything weird was weird. Now I know that it is the people that call others weird that are weird."

"The long and winding road that leads to your door / Will never disappear, / I've seen that road before it always leads me here, / Leads me to your door."

"I love to hear a choir. I love the humanity, to see the faces of real people devoting themselves to a piece of music. I like the teamwork. It makes me feel optimistic about the human race when I see them cooperating like that."
"I don't take me seriously. If we get some giggles, I don't mind."

"I was afraid to take my suit off in case I got raped. But I knew you had to keep your spirits up. So I organized sing-songs."
"We didn't all get into music for a job! We got into music to avoid a job, in truth—and get lots of girls."

Song: From Maybe I'm Amazed

Maybe I'm a man and maybe I'm a lonely man
Who's in the middle of something
That he doesn't really understand.

Maybe I'm a man and maybe you're the only woman
Who could ever help me.
Baby, won't you help me understand?

Maybe I'm amazed at the way you're with me all the time.
Maybe I'm afraid of the way I leave you.
Maybe I'm amazed at the way you help me sing my song,
Right me when I'm wrong.
Maybe I'm amazed at the way I really need you.

Doris Day

"If it's true that men are such beasts, this must account for the fact that most women are animal lovers."
"The really frightening thing about middle age is the knowledge that you'll grow out of it."

Liberace

"I had to dare a little bit. Who am I kidding? I had to dare a lot."
"Don't wear one ring, wear five or six. People ask how I can play with all those rings, and I reply, 'Very well, thank you.'"

"I cried all the way to the bank."

"You know that bank I used to cry all the way to? I bought it."

Elizabeth Taylor:

"Everything makes me nervous—except making films."

"I am a very committed wife. And I should be committed too—for being married so many times."

"I don't pretend to be an ordinary housewife."

"I feel very adventurous. There are so many doors to be opened, and I'm not afraid to look behind them."

"I fell off my pink cloud with a thud."

"I have a woman's body and a child's emotions."

"Richard [Burton] is a very sexy man. He's got that sort of jungle essence that one can sense."

" So much to do, so little done, such things to be."

"I think I'm finally growing up—and about time."

"Some of my best leading men have been dogs and horses."

"The problem with people who have no vices is that generally you can be pretty sure they're going to have some pretty annoying virtues."

"I've always admitted that I'm ruled by my passions."

Marilyn Monroe:

"Being a sex symbol is a heavy load to carry, especially when one is tired, hurt, and bewildered."

"Fame will go by and, so long, I've had you, fame. If it goes by, I've always known it was fickle. So at least it's something I experience, but that's not where I live."

"I have too many fantasies to be a housewife. I guess I am a fantasy."

"I don't mind living in a man's world as long as I can be a woman in it."

Cher:
"I'm insecure about everything, because... I'm never going to look in the mirror and see this blond, blue-eyed girl. That is my idea of what I'd like to look like."

"I'm still friends with all my exes, apart from my husbands."

"I've always taken risks and never worried what the world might really think of me."

"If you really want something, you can figure out how to make it happen."

"I can trust my friends. These people force me to examine myself, encourage me to grow."

The Raft in my life is Dina, my oldest daughter. Dina is truly a gentle, loving spirit who is definitely her own person. She met her husband Michael while they were both saving kittens in New York City. Dina is also an herbalist—she studies herbs and their healing abilities, and she makes all of us teas to drink to cure us when we have an ailment. Dina has her nursing degree and loves helping people. She can become completely engrossed in whatever she is doing; it is sensation and experience that guides her. She follows her own impulses and is adaptable. Dina loves living on her own time clock and doesn't let herself be hurried or interrupted by time constraints. Waiting for her to get ready to go someplace can be an all-day event, especially if she becomes distracted by something that catches her eye, like a book on herbs or a gerbil that needs attention. At that point, she will become so engaged in the herbs or the gerbil that she forgets about getting ready! But her kindness, generosity, and loving heart make her worth the wait.

In a job, you will have to teach a raft what to do; he will gladly follow wherever you lead, as long as you do not try to control him. They value freedom and being their own person. They will do things in their own time frame. They enjoy working in an atmosphere that allows them to do the things that feel "harmonious" to them. Once they find that job, it becomes a vocation and not merely a job. An example of this would be Fox Mulder on *The X-Files*. He values the freedom to do what he wants to do, the things that feel harmonious to his values and beliefs. Control would not work well with Fox Mulder, and indeed it has not. A Raft does not adapt well where there are rigid job schedules, rules, and regulations; they are drawn to careers where there is creative expression, caretaking professions (but being introverts, they need to work more one–on-one than in settings where they would interact with large amounts of people), adventure, or in areas where they can express themselves physically—for example, working with their hands. Remember, they learn by *doing*.

As a friend, a Raft can be fun because they are in the "here and now" and will be willing to go wherever you want to go. They are extremely creative and imaginative, and they have a novel approach to life. As their friend, you will be the current that takes them in a specific direction. If you have a Raft friend, you need to be careful where your waves may take them. They can also be emotionally moody at times. They have a strong sense of faithfulness and loyalty, and they tend to develop intense and devoted friendships. An introvert's loyalty and feelings are not diminished by time and distance, which can be a surprise and an enigma to their extroverted friends, Their feelings are deeper and more lasting, which is why a violation of trust can be so devastating for an introvert.

In a relationship, a Raft is wonderful when you want to just relax and enjoy yourself with no purpose or goals in mind, just a laid-back, relaxed, "let's see where this takes us" attitude. Marriage to a Raft transforms you into the protector, with much of the responsibility falling on your shoulders. Hopefully, the Raft is not the breadwinner in the relationship. If this is the case, you are in for a very unpredictable and unnerving ride, because a raft has no way to steer. If you are the breadwinner and your partner is the Raft, the experience can be more peaceful. The Raft can even help you to relax and take life easier and enjoy the scenery on your course through life.

Sometimes, a Raft will discover who they really are and want to become that person, and it's hard for the "guide" to let go of their position as protector. This is a time to step back and encourage instead of feeling threatened. It's an illuminating experience to watch a Raft transform into their purpose, kind of like watching a butterfly in metamorphosis.

Rafts have a very difficult time expressing anger. It may not be an easy task to find out what is bothering them because they don't want to make waves in their relationships. It will take a lot of patience on the partner's part and a lot of trust on their part. Once trust has been found to be misplaced, you will be shut out, and that trust will not be readily earned again.

What a Raft needs from you:

- Listen attentively to them.

- Encourage their interests and activities.

- Allow them to keep their options open.

- Work on chores together.

- Respect their privacy.

- Be specific when you want them to do something that is important to you.

- Give them plenty of time.

- Make everything fun.

You'll notice that your Raft is overwhelmed if they begin analyzing a situation, adopt a "take charge" attitude, or begin to make critical comments toward you. You can help them through this turmoil by helping them to look at the problem or situation more objectively, so they can see that they need to stop and take care of themselves.

If you are a Raft and can see that you are becoming overwhelmed, what you can do for yourself is to cut down on your commitments to helping others and look at the situation in a logical way—even making lists when necessary. Sometimes, finding an outlet that involves your analytical mind can also be beneficial, because it gets your focus off the situation.

Exercises that can be helpful:

Learn to take care of your body with energy healing (Reiki, Qui Gong), and practice meditation, tai chi, or yoga to renew your energy.

Pay attention to your imagination and your fantasies. Are you using them to energize your feelings? What are you saying to yourself about a topic, a person, a situation? What purpose is your fantasy, or self-talk, serving?

During extreme stress, crisis, or grief, a Raft needs direction. They will tend to move from one subject or project to the next, being unable to focus their thoughts on one topic for any length of time. They need assistance from the people in their life to keep them on track. Help them to feel their feelings and make small decisions in their life. Sometimes just helping to structure the day can be a big benefit to a grief-stricken Raft.

Rafts tend to discover their spirituality in solitude. Examples would be in a park, at a petting zoo, or near bodies of water (e.g. beach, river, lake, or pond). Also in places with a person, child, or animal, that is close to them, sharing confidences. If they do attend spiritual practices in a group setting, they tend to stay in the background. As they mature in their spirituality, they realize that their purpose is to experience the world through activities and sensations, to grow, and to share their understanding with others.

"I am thankful for

My cooperative and considerate nature
My enjoyment of life's precious moments
My capacity to minister to the hurts I see
The ways in which I bring harmony to human endeavors

In the storms of life, I can find shelter by

Accomplishing something that enhances my faith in myself
Being in the world of nature to experience God at work in this world
Assessing what really happened in tough situations in an objective way, thereby giving myself a fresh start

To honor myself and my pathway to God, I can

Allow myself time to be spiritual in my own way
Clarify my values so that I can know best how to serve others
Define and accept a logical basis for what I take on faith in order to communicate it more easily to others" *Soul Types*, page 285

ISFP Prayer: Lord, help me to stand up for my rights (if you don't mind my asking or think I'm interfering).

Section 4
SJs—Traditionalists

These are the people who have a strong work ethic and sense of duty. They value the importance of having rules, standards, or guidelines, and they fully support the people and authority systems that enforce them. Traditionalists make sure that everything that should get done, does get done. And they want not only to make sure that things get done, but to make sure that they are done in the "right" way. Keirsey calls them "Guardians," the Tiegers call them "Traditionalists," and maybe they can best be described as "Guardians of Tradition." They are people of habit who like to follow the established routines and traditions, and they become Guardians in order to ensure that no one is allowed in who will disrupt those routines or traditions. I have a friend who is a Traditionalist, and I once heard him comment that our political system had always worked for him and that he trusted in a system that had always worked.

They are especially attracted to sayings from the past, and you will find that they tend to manage their behaviors on guidelines that have *always worked* in the past. They are more likely to look back in time and long for the way things "used to be." In their family and personal relationships, the Guardians have a deep sense of responsibility and obligation. They see themselves as the "stewards," the "keepers," the "protectors" of the family. They will feel extreme guilt if they feel they have not fulfilled their duty, their responsibility, in a proper manner.

As in all the other types, there are two types of Guardians, one which is more directive, and the other which is more nurturing. The directive Guardians feel it is their place to get everyone else into shape and show them what they "should" do. The nurturing Guardian sees their role as caretaker and nurturer, ensuring that that the family unit is provided for and that nothing breaks it apart. In *The Pygmalion Project*, Stephen Montgomery refers to Lucy as the directive Guardian and Charlie Brown as the nurturing Guardian. Can you see the difference in Lucy's and Charlie Brown's approaches in following traditions?

In romance, the Guardian is the personality style with the strongest commitment to the family in the traditional sense of the word. They are marriage-minded and are often the long-suffering partner who will sacrifice their own happiness for the sake of the family.

The Traditionalists are:

ESTJ—Patrol Boat

ISTJ—Canoe

ESFJ—Cargo Ship

ISFJ—Tugboat

ESTJ Extroverted Thinking/Introverted Sensing

PATROL BOAT

Their theme is Supervisor/Implementation. They thrive on organization and follow-through. Their goals are to see that things are done correctly and to be useful to others. Their driving force is their need to analyze and bring into logical order the people, activities, and things in their lives. They are "take-charge" kind of people, and they know what everybody else should be doing too. Their motto is, "Somebody has to take charge to get things done right."

I chose a Patrol Boat to represent the Supervisor/Implementer because it is a no-nonsense boat that patrols the waterways making sure that all the other boats follow the rules. They step in and get the job done. They wish to be useful. They want things to be done "right"—meaning *their* way. They do not always understand that there can be exceptions to the rules. They believe you follow the rules at all costs!

These are the stable, no-frills people that you will meet in your life. There are a lot of these people; they are the backbone of our lives. Many times, they accomplish the necessary details so that others can acquire the limelight. But other times, they take control of the limelight themselves—especially if someone else is doing it the wrong way. Because they believe that they know the right way to do things, they are sometimes guilty of jumping to conclusions too quickly. They have a very strong sense of principles and try to live up to the rules they have set for themselves, expecting others to also abide by those rules even though others may not be aware of what those rules are.

When I look back, I believe that Robert Kennedy was a Patrol Boat for his brother, John F. Kennedy. Of course, Robert Kennedy became a different type of boat in later years, but a Patrol Boat was the nature of his being an aide to his brother. He was the "man behind the man," who did the things that helped make his brother great, the one who watched the waters and made sure that things were done properly. After the death of President Kennedy, Robert Kennedy retired his Patrol Boat and developed a great fleet of his own. It was a tragedy his fleet was sunk before we had the opportunity to learn its potential.

Another example of a Patrol Boat personality would be Lucy van Pelt (as mentioned earlier) in *Peanuts*. Lucy forever knows what Charlie Brown should do and the way he should do it. Lucy is very strong-willed and has an intense need to be in control. Also, Bette Davis and Barbara Stanwyck are listed as being representatives of this style. Both women were no-nonsense type of people, who were extremely efficient, thorough, fearless, and iron-willed. They took every role they played seriously and approached them in a disciplined and consistent manner.

> **Bette Davis:** Although she earned a reputation for being difficult to work with, Bette set a new precedent for women.
> "She sure knew how to be Bette Davis. She was cantankerous and flamboyant, but I also thought there was an undercurrent of playfulness to her behavior."

Regarding smoking:

"I Do Not Wish To Be Told What To Do!

"I wish to have my own life. All this whole thing has to do with people who gave up smoking and can't stand it! I think it's a big farce myself. And I think it's our own business what we do. Who has the right to say 'You can't smoke'? Makes me smoke *more*! Ha-*ha*-ha. No. I don't like it."

After surviving a stroke, a mastectomy, four marriages, more than fifty years in the movie business, and almost eighty years on the planet, Bette Davis knows exactly who she is and what she does not like.

She once sued Warner Bros., the studio that had her under contract, because the men who ran it tried to make her play parts she thought weren't right for her. They tried to put her in pictures she didn't like. And that just made Miss Davis not want to do them *more*!

At one time, the actress who won Oscars for *Dangerous* in 1935 and *Jezebel* in 1938 had quite a reputation for being difficult—

"At one time?!" she erupts. "I've been known as difficult for fifty years, practically! What do you mean 'at one time'?! Nooo, I've been like this for fifty years. And it's always always to make it the best film I can make it!"

Miss Davis has a very strong sense of right and wrong, of what is proper and what is not.

When she concludes a sentence by punctuating it with "Right," or "Yes" or "No" or "Definitely"—biting the words hard so that they snap off brittlely at the end—you know that the matter at hand has been disposed of to her satisfaction. Subject closed. That's it. Next question.

Bette Davis defiantly scrunches and twists another filter tip into the ashtray. She smiles as she lights up another cigarette and shoots a plume of smoke into the air, as if into the face of some wicked man, coolly blowing him away.

End of topic.

Meeting Miss Davis by Jim Emerson

Quotes from Bette Davis:
"It has been my experience that one cannot, in any shape or form, depend on human relations for lasting reward. It is only work that truly satisfies."

"I was thought to be 'stuck up.' I wasn't. I was just sure of myself. This is and always has been an unforgivable quality to the unsure."

"Love is not enough. It must be the foundation, the cornerstone—but not the complete structure. It is much too pliable, too yielding."

John Wayne:
Courage is being scared to death … and saddling up anyway.

"When you come slam bang up against trouble, it never looks half as bad if you face up to it."

"I have tried to live my life so that my family would love me and my friends respect me. The others can do whatever the hell they please."

"A man's got to have a code, a creed to live by, no matter his job."

"I've always followed my father's advice: he told me, first to always keep my word, and second, to never insult anybody unintentionally. If I insult you, you can be goddamn sure I intend to. And, third, he told me not to go around looking for trouble."

"I've always had deep faith that there is a Supreme Being, there has to be. To me, that's just a normal thing, to have that kind of faith. The fact that He's let me stick around a little longer, or She's let me stick around a little longer, certainly goes great with me—

and I want to hang around as long as I'm healthy and not in anybody's way."

"We've made mistakes along the way, but that's no reason to start tearing up the best flag God ever gave to any country."

"I am a demonstrative man, a baby-picker-upper, a hugger and a kisser—that's my nature."

"Sure, I wave the American flag. Do you know a better flag to wave? Sure, I love my country, with all her faults. I'm not ashamed of that, never have been, never will be. I was proud when President Nixon ordered the mining of Haiphong Harbor, which we should have done long ago, because I think we're helping a brave little country defend herself against Communist invasion."

"If everything isn't black and white, I say, why the hell not?"

"The West—the very words go straight to that place of the heart where Americans feel the spirit of pride in their western heritage—the triumph of personal courage over any obstacle, whether nature or man."

"You know, I hear everybody talking about the generation gap. Frankly, sometimes I don't know what they're talking about. Heck, by now I should know a little bit about it, if I'm ever going to. I have seven kids and eighteen grandkids, and I don't seem to have any trouble talking to any of them. Never have had, and I don't intend to start now."

"I can tell you why I love her. I have a lust for her dignity. I look at her wonderfully classic face, and I see hidden in it a sense of humor that I love. I think of wonderful, exciting, decent things when I look at her...."

"There've been a lot of stories about how I got to be called Duke. One was that I played the part of a duke in a school play—which I never did. Sometimes they even said I was descended from royalty! It was all a lot of rubbish. Hell, the truth is that I was named after a dog!"

"Women have the right to work wherever they want, as long as they have the dinner ready when you get home."

"A man ought to do what he thinks is right."

"A horse is a horse—it ain't make a difference what color it is."

"Talk low, talk slow, and don't say too much."

"I stick to simple themes. Love. Hate. No nuances. I stay away from psychoanalyst's couch scenes. Couches are good for one thing."

"Never say sorry—it's a sign of weakness."

Barbara Stanwyck:

"Stanwyck was sassy and gave lots of lip; you got the impression she could hold her own with just about anyone. And sure enough, she applied her tart tongue, nimble wit, and precision timing to scripts by some of Hollywood's most linguistically agile screenwriters, from Preston Sturges to Billy Wilder."

"Stanwyck was uncommonly beloved by those at the bottom of the studio hierarchy for being unmannered, non-temperamental, and down-to-earth."

"Tough, strong, and smart, but no less feminine than some of her screwball sisters, she has learned to survive in a cut-throat world, living by her wits. She's at her best when she's in control, and she usually is."

"She was no glamour girl; she seemed much too savvy, practical, and natural for that sort of vanity.

She knew the gaffers on her pictures, remembered their names, and often spent time chatting with the crew between takes.
Stanwyck could make you believe she was part of the everyday world we all live in, not just a fantasy on the silver screen. She could easily be the woman down the aisle in the supermarket, driving that car in the next lane, or working in the office down the hall. While other stars went for the 'larger than life' roles, Stanwyck—as an all-American working girl or a cunning seductress—generally kept her feet planted firmly on the ground."

Barbara Stanwyck: Working Girl, Movie Star
by Jim Emerson

Quotes from Barbara Stanwyck:
"Career is too pompous a word. It was a job, and I have always felt privileged to be paid for what I love doing."

Bruce Willis:
"I'm staggered by the question of what it's like to be a multimillionaire. I always have to remind myself that I am."

"My wife heard me say 'I love you' a thousand times, but she never once heard me say 'sorry.'"

"I like having the dough to come and go as I please."

"On the one hand, we'll never experience childbirth. On the other hand, we can open all our own jars."

"You can't undo the past... but you can certainly not repeat it."

Linda Branham M.Ed.

Raymond Burr:
"Try and live your life the way you wish other people would live theirs."

In my office, Marietta is the Patrol Boat. She keeps everyone on task. One of her favorite things to do is to rearrange the office supplies so that she is the only one who knows where they are, and we all have to go to her to find them. Marietta is very vocal about speaking up for the injustices she sees in the world, but she is also always ready to lend a hand to see that those injustices are addressed. She rolls up her sleeves and tackles the problem to *her* satisfaction. When she went through a very stressful time in her life, I saw her become rigid and structured in the way she organized the office and her home life. Then, as her life became more stable, she relaxed more and learned to accept herself more.

As she has started making home visits and working individually with families, it has been interesting to hear her description of the family situation (remember, we work with child abuse and neglect families). She sees the situations as very cut-and-dried, black-and-white, and is very quick to let families know what they need to do to straighten themselves out!

In the workforce, you'll find that Patrol Boats are the ones who see that the job gets job done the way it is "supposed" to be done, the ones in the background that everyone else depends on. They circle the situation making sure everyone does their job—and they can be very outspoken and direct when they see someone not doing what they are "supposed" to be doing.

A Patrol Boat can always be counted on to follow projects through to completion; they will continue patrolling the waters, keeping their eyes on the goal, while the Runabout/Speedboat is busy running around in circles making waves and creating chaos. They have no patience with inefficiency and will stay with the task until it is completed. The negative side is they can become too rigid and detail-oriented and end up hurting the feelings of their coworkers. They believe they are the only ones who know how to get things done correctly, and they are quick to point it out to others. They don't understand that a choice can be subjective—to them, it is either the way they want it done, or it's wrong.

They need a sense of the predictable in their lives. They will not begin a new project until they have plan they feel will work. Then they divide a project down into a series of steps and complete these steps in a specified order. They have a very systematic approach to getting things done.

In a relationship, you'll find the Patrol Boat will sometimes be behind the person who is "out front," so to speak. When one of the partners is a Patrol Boat, that person will be the one who does the basic, behind-the-scenes work making sure that everything gets done "right," which frees the other one to do the exciting jobs. In a relationship with a Patrol Boat, the essentials will always be completed; all of your basic needs will be met. They can become the "Protector" in a relationship, making sure that their partner has everything they need and are well looked after. Their downside is that they are not always aware of other people's feelings; they are so busy taking care of the details and the specifics that feelings and emotions can go unnoticed. So if you are in a relationship with a Patrol Boat, you may have to help them become aware that feelings are also important to you. And always show them how grateful you are for their practical and loyal caretaking, and how well they look out for you.

What a Patrol Boat needs from you:

- Express your gratitude.

- Listen to the advice they share with you for your own good.

- Respect their need to control things.

- Don't mess up or change their routines.

- Be very straightforward and give specific details when discussing problems.

- Appeal to their sense of fairness when attempting to reason with them.

- Don't be put off by their frankness; they are merely sharing their perception of the world with you.

When you notice that your Patrol Boat is becoming hypersensitive, acting irritated, or concentrating too hard on a project, they may be feeling overwhelmed. You can help them by giving them some practical, detailed suggestions, or by offering alternatives that may be helpful to whatever they are doing.

If you are a Patrol Boat and notice yourself becoming overwhelmed and find yourself being highly controlling or quick to anger, you may want to follow some of the suggestions below:

- Walk away when you become angry.

- Make sure you understand the facts being presented to you.

- Be open to learning new ways of looking at things.

- Remember that some people do not come from a logical, direct framework like you do.

- Become familiar with your inner voice that judges what "should" be done.

- Let others help you, and let them do it their way.

- Learn to look at and understand the process of your anger. Do you hold it in your body? Where in your body? Do you get headaches?

Exercises that may be helpful:

Keep a journal and write down how many times a day you are disappointed, either with yourself or with others around you. What are the "rules" you are using to determine that someone has disappointed you? What are the rules that you feel you have failed to live up to?

In your journal, take the opposing view to your normal position. Argue *for* something that you are usually against.

During times of extreme stress, crisis, or grief, a Patrol Boat needs structure in order to feel grounded. Helping them to set a schedule where there is predictability back in their lives is extremely important. Then they need to learn how to look at their feelings about whatever the situation is. Looking at feelings is not an easy task for a Patrol Boat; in fact, some are unable to do it. Looking at feelings and different approaches to their normal, logical one can completely undermine a Patrol Boat's sense of their worldview. So this is an area where you need to tread softly. When they are able to see that there is a differing worldview that is truly acceptable, they can become more balanced individuals and less rigid in their approach to what is right and what is wrong. So help them look at the personal meaning behind their experience, and to look at the impact it may also have on those closest to them.

Crisis can plunge a Patrol Boat into a window of experience where they have never gone before. Experiencing their feelings in such a manner can cause them to come face-to-face with their faith. Here is where they can develop a authentic sense of belief that will override their previous sense of control.

Before a crisis, spirituality for a Patrol Boat is common-sense and purposeful. They want to get together with other Patrol Boats and help the larger community who, in their estimation, needs their assistance. Patrol Boats will be the staunch supporters of church doctrines and dogma, keeping everyone focused on upholding their disciplined standards of conduct. As they mature spiritually, they begin to relax and see that everything is happening for the best, that there is a greater design that they are unaware of—they will begin to relax their rules and enjoy watching life unfold on its own. A crisis can take them here more quickly and more deeply.

"I am thankful for

> My orientation toward fairness and justice
> My sense of order and responsibility
> My ability to lead others and accomplish goals
> The decisiveness and reasoning I bring to solving problems

In the storms of life, I can find shelter by

> Focusing on what truly matters to me, both now and for eternity
> Embracing instead of avoiding my emotions, realizing that feelings can enrich my life
> Taking time alone to ensure that *all* my needs are met

To honor myself and my pathway to God, I can

> Find tangible ways to incorporate the spiritual into my daily life
> Use my organizational gifts to be a part of something that matters
> Value the intangible—my relationships and other areas that give meaning to life" *Soul Types*, page 187–188

ESTJ Prayer: God, help me to not try to *run* everything. But, if You need some help, just ask!

ISTJ Introverted Sensing/Extroverted Thinking

CANOE

The Canoe's theme is Planner/Monitor/Inspector. They thrive on being careful and sensible. They value hard work and honesty and are distrustful of new ideas. They are practical, dependable, and loyal. Their driving force is their sense of responsibility for doing what needs to be done. Their goal is to get the job done, one step at a time. Their slogan might be, "Say what you mean and mean what you say."

I used a canoe to represent the Planner/Monitor because a canoe is stable, careful, sensible, more individualistic, practical, and dependable. A canoe works on its own, in a quiet manner, to get the job done. It takes its time and handles all of the details. It goes its own way and takes its own time, but reaches its objective. They take their work seriously and want others to do the same. They are very conscientious in their approach to their work, especially if details involving data and numbers are concerned. Then they can become painstakingly thorough.

Canoe personalities prefer simplicity, freedom, and mobility. They can be similar to a Sailboat in some areas, but they prefer the inner areas of life, whereas a sailboat likes the open sea. They like to explore in chartered areas, not in the unknown. They are extremely individualistic. They are more loners and isolated than Sailboats. They prefer to travel light, without a lot of personal effects to cramp their style. They can maneuver well in the unstable waters of crisis and demanding times. They are both uncomplicated and natural. They do tend to be very literal in their understanding of life, and this can cause them to misinterpret others around them—especially people, or boats, who are less focused and detail-oriented.

They are not always sure what the other people in their workplace want of them. They tend to keep their ironic humor to themselves unless they are with very close friends or family. They have learned that not everyone sees a situation the same way that they do, and so they become reluctant to share their views with others. They can become particularly indecisive when they feel they do not have sufficient information or facts to make a qualified decision. If they feel slighted at work, they can become easily hurt, and when a Canoe feels unappreciated, others will notice. They become aloof and distant. When this happens, they can become very inflexible and dig in their heels because they are sure that their ideas about what needs to be done are absolutely correct, and they will find the rules, in writing, to prove their point. In the literature the examples listed are George H. W. Bush, Evander Holyfield, Julia Roberts, Gary Sinise, Kirk Douglas, and the fictional Joe Friday. Upon researching Evander Holyfield, I found that he has been very thorough, single-focused, steadfast, and responsible in his approach to boxing; he has also remained a very private person in the midst of his fame and wins in his boxing career.

President George H. W. Bush was known to be practical, dependable, loyal to his beliefs, responsible to his position, and detail-oriented. He valued hard work and honesty in his no-nonsense approach to being President of the United States. These are all examples of the behavior and approach to life of a Canoe personality.

President George H. W. Bush:
"America needs to be more like the Waltons."
"America today is a proud, free nation, decent and civil, a place we cannot help but love. We know in our hearts, not loudly and proudly, but as a simple fact, that this country has meaning beyond what we see, and that our strength is a force for good."
"We cannot hope only to leave our children a bigger car, a bigger bank account. We must hope to give them a sense of what it means to be a loyal friend, a loving parent, a citizen who leaves his home, his neighborhood, and town better than he found it."
"We live in a peaceful, prosperous time, but we can make it better."

Evander Holyfield:
"Well, I always knew that the best fighter would get into the hall of fame. There was no doubt in [my] mind that I would get there. I really would rather get in there the right way and be happy once I get there, because that means it's the end of your career and there are other things."

"My goal is to be the undisputed Heavyweight Champion of the World."

"No. I probably do better not being in politics. They have too much control over you when you are in politics."

"I happened to have the courage to go out there and give it my best shot."

"Well, when I think of steroids, I think of an image. You have the advantage over someone, which is a form of cheating. I guess it wouldn't be right unless it was legal for everybody. Reason it's not legal for everybody is because it can hurt people seriously."

Julia Roberts:
"I guess what I like the least about this is would be that there doesn't seem to be too much interest or room for the simple truth."

"I just think that in the big scheme of the world, the way media deals with people in show business, is that the fiction it fodders is so salivated after, and so the simple truth doesn't really seem to serve much of a purpose."

"If you love someone, you say it, right then, out loud. Otherwise, the moment just passes you by."

"I'm an utterly average, total geek."

"You know it's love when all you want is that person to be happy, even if you're not part of their happiness."

"True love doesn't come to you—it has to be inside you."

"Anyone who doesn't make mistakes isn't trying hard enough."

" I don't get angry very often. I lose my temper rarely. And when I do, there's always a legitimate cause."

"You can be true to the character all you want, but you've got to go home with yourself."

Gary Sinise:
"But I've got more to learn, too. I don't feel like I'm done or I know it all."

"I save money when I'm working so that I never have to take a role simply to pay the bills."

"It's a Hollywood creation—part actual research, development, and science, and part movie."

"Since I've had kids, I haven't read a huge lot of classics. I've been too busy. It now takes me about a year to read a book."

"When I think of work, it's mostly about having control over your destiny, as opposed to being at the mercy of what's out there."

"Yeah, I volunteered to support the troops, and get out there and show them that we care about them."

Kirk Douglas:
"If you want to know about a man, you can find out an awful lot by looking at who he married."

'Life is like a B-picture script! It is that corny. If I had my life story offered to me to film, I'd turn it down."

"When you become a star, you don't change—everyone else does."

"Why can't a woman be more like a dog, huh? So sweet, loving, attentive."

"The older you get, the more awards you get. So, if you live long enough, then you get all the awards eventually."

Joe Friday:
Jack Webb as Joe Friday was sensible, to the point, detail-oriented, dependable, and able to "get the job done" no matter what situation arose.

Sherri is a Canoe friend of mine. She is a very good friend and a co-worker, so I know her in several different roles. Sherri is quiet, yet also strong-willed. She is down-to-earth, practical, meticulous, and extremely dependable. She is my Assistant Supervisor in the office, and I know I can count on her to be accurate, thorough, and to get the job done. Since we work on a contract with Child Protective Services, accuracy and detail are important. And my being an INFP (Nautilus) does not really lend itself to a detail orientation. Sherri is the one who faithfully sees that the government rules and guidelines are followed, keeping me and all of the in-home consultants on track. As a friend, Sherri is warm, caring, and has always been there for me. She is very private, and is cautious about letting other people into her life. She has also been that dependable, supportive, down-to-earth Canoe that provides common sense and stability during my times of turbulent waters.

If you are in a working situation with a Canoe, their greatest potential is in unstable or uncharted areas. Many politicians use this expertise well. A Canoe individual would be able to help the politician be able to navigate quietly and quickly through the shallow waters of public opinion and scrutiny. Imagine the difference in our history books if Nixon had used a canoe at Watergate instead of a submarine. A canoe is quiet and quick; a submarine is seen as a full-fledged attack of secrecy.

As friends, Canoes are calm and easygoing. They don't carry a lot of baggage with them, preferring to experience life as it occurs, unencumbered. These are the friends who are dependable, loyal, and responsible, but need their space to be alone. These are the people who live "in the now." They can be very spiritual in that they are very much in touch with who they are and don't depend on others to define themselves. If you have a Canoe friend, when you are in a time of a crisis, they will come in quietly and swiftly, doing what needs to be done, and then be on their way again to quieter waters.

If you are considering a relationship with a Canoe, be aware that they don't like a lot of baggage or clutter. If you don't mind living life without a lot of "things," you may be able to find space with a Canoe.

You will need to allow and respect the alone time that a Canoe needs. They are very private individuals, and they guard their feelings and emotions from others. This relationship will be a celebration of the love of the simple pleasures of life and nature. They will put out a lot of energy to keep their home and family running smoothly.

What a Canoe needs from you:

- Listen to them attentively.

- Show your appreciation for their hard work.

- Respect their need for order and routines.

- Give them time to think about things before being ready to discuss them.

- When discussing any problems, remain calm, be specific and detail-oriented, and above all else, be honest. Give them plenty of facts to make it clear.

- Respect their need for privacy.

Be alert to when the Canoe is feeling overwhelmed. They will start to have difficulties handling the everyday details and specifics, and will be unable to focus clearly. You may notice that they are worrying obsessively or acting impulsively, both completely out of their usual nature. They can become extremely hurt by criticism or rejection because they have a high need to feel valued and appreciated.

During these times, you can help the Canoe by:

- Help them to see that others are looking at things differently than they do.

- Convince them to take time for themselves to relax.

- Help them with some of the tasks or duties that they feel have to be done.

If you are a Canoe and are feeling overwhelmed with circumstances in your life, becoming moody and withdrawn, here are some things that you can do:

- Concentrate on the big picture. Ask yourself what will really be important in the long term—for example, five years from now.

- Imagine the worst thing that could happen, and then plan for what you would do in that situation.

- Listen to other people's ideas entirely before you pass judgment on them; make sure you really understand their ideas, or what they are really saying.

- Let other people help you.

- Find someone you can be open with, someone you can trust.

- Take the time to be aware of the other person—what they are feeling, where they are coming from, what their expectations are.

- Accept that your approach to life, to circumstances, is unique, and learn to adapt your strengths to others' views, and you will find that nothing is impossible for you.

Exercises that can be helpful:

When you find yourself becoming overwhelmed about a goal you have set for yourself, *stop*—and ask yourself if the goal is really worth the level of upsetness you are feeling. What are you saying to yourself?

For a few days, whenever you find yourself becoming self-righteous or judgmental, *stop*—and make a list of what standards you are measuring the person against. Then look at these standards and evaluate how they are affecting the relationships in your life.

In a crisis situation, Canoes will act as if they are caught in a whirlpool with no way out. They will begin to circle around and around the problem to understand it, but feel themselves getting pulled in even further. This is a time when talking to someone else can be an important step in getting out of the circular thoughts. Activities with friends can be helpful because they also take you out of those circular patterns. Canoes especially can get lost in their own thoughts and need support from others during times of crisis. And unfortunately, this is when they most seclude themselves and try to do it alone. So if you have a friend who is a Canoe who is experiencing a crisis, try to get them out of the whirlpools in their mind and focus on life in the external world.

Canoes approach spirituality in a way where they can see tangible results. They see what works in the lives of others and adapt these results in their own spiritual path. Canoes like to apply the principles that they have learned to situations in their daily lives. So as the waters become hazardous around them, they will reach back and pull out the specifics of their own past experiences, or what they have seen to be helpful to others in similar circumstances, and apply it in the moment. Integrity and truth are the characteristics of a Canoe finding spiritual awareness. Everything will just seem to flow effortlessly, and they will just seem to know what to do and when.

"I am thankful for

My gifts of sensibility and logic
My awareness of the merit of learning from and building on past experiences
My ability to follow through on commitments
The ease with which I handle details and facts

In the storms of life, I can find shelter by

Looking for guidance from what has worked before and how things are resolved through faith

Turning over some of my responsibilities to others

Asking for help to assess the big picture—the larger meaning

To honor myself and my pathway to God, I can

Seek the practices that fit into my routine

Understand and apply unchanging truths in this changing world

Explore other traditions or spiritual disciplines to open the boundaries of my soul without violating what I know to be true"

Soul Types, page 87

ISTJ Prayer: Lord, help me to relax about insignificant details, beginning tomorrow at 9:31:16 A.M. EST.

ESFJ Extroverted Feeling/Introverted Sensing

CARGO SHIP

The theme of a Cargo ship is Providing/Caretaker. They thrive on being needed and helping others. Their goal is to ensure that physical needs are met. They have a genuine concern for the needs of others, and their main focus is to support and supply others with what they need. Their driving forces are strong caring about other people and their hands-on approach to help others. Their motto is "I wear many hats."

I chose a Cargo Ship to represent this personality because a Cargo ship carries big loads for other people; they provide the necessities of life for others. A Cargo Ship personality is eager to take care of others and make sure they are supplied with all of the necessities of life. They are dependable; their favorite thing to do is to serve other people. They bring an atmosphere of warmth to everything that they do.

You can easily spot a Cargo Ship because they will be talkative and concerned about the other person. They are very expressive and enthusiastic, and they will talk about their personal values. They will also make sure that you have everything that you need.

Cargo ships are useful for long journeys. They are dependable and can carry large loads. This type of person has a job to do, and they get it done. They are hard workers. Cargo ships are the caretakers who carry the load for everyone else. They tend to be very efficient and single-minded. They make up their own minds about what should be accomplished and work toward it steadily, regardless of protests or distractions. Descriptive words would be organized, practical, dependable, realistic, and responsible. They do expect payment, not necessarily in money, but in like services or loyalty. Cargo Ships are very traditional people who value family and friends and give freely of themselves.

They are terrific at networking in a place of business and are very good in getting others on board in a cooperative manner. They are extremely good for advocating for the needs of those less fortunate. They can get into trouble, though, when they slight their own personal needs in favor of the high standards that they set for themselves.

They are well organized. They have strong values and work ethic, and they follow the rules. They are planners. They are dependable, have genuine concern for the needs of others, like routine, and dislike change. They are responsible, conservative, friendly, nurturing, and conscientious. They have a good sense of space and function.

Do you know anyone who fits the description of a Cargo Ship? I can think of a whole list of people right now. Many members of Al-anon would recognize themselves in this description. Maybe we could start a whole new support group just for Cargo Ships! The principles of Al-anon would be useful for these people: keep the focus on you, and don't try to do for others what they are capable of doing for themselves. It's okay to help people who have legitimate needs, or as an act of kindness. But it's not okay to help someone who simply doesn't want to be responsible for, or carry, his or her own load. If you are a Cargo Ship, it's good to stop and ask yourself if this is a legitimate need, or if you are doing something that the other person is capable of doing for themselves—something that is their responsibility.

The Cargo Ship in our office is Stephanie, and she is so very much a Cargo Ship it is amazing. She is extremely good at networking and will put her job ahead of her own needs. She has very high standards of how she lives and behaves, and sometimes overwhelms herself with responsibilities of caretaking in her life. I remember one family Stephanie was working with during Christmas, who called her on Christmas Eve to have Stephanie bring her a broom. Now, we do make home visits over the holidays, but only in a crisis. Needing a broom is not a crisis. But Stephanie was going to take the lady a broom on Christmas Eve—until I stopped her. That is very typical behavior for a Cargo Ship: responsible, nurturing, dependable, and conscientious.

I see these people as the strong, silent type—not *just* the caretakers, but more like the characters portrayed by John Wayne, even though John Wayne himself is a Patrol Boat. They are caring, compassionate, and dependable.

Examples of Cargo Ships in the literature are:

> **Mary Tyler Moore:**
> "I'm an experienced woman; I've been around . . . well, all right, I might not've been around, but I've been . . . nearby."
> "In recent years she has dedicated herself to improving the lives of people with disabilities and with changing the way we think about animals in our society. She has served as the spokesperson for the Juvenile Diabetes Association (JDF) since 1985 and works actively in conjunction with government and the research community to improve the lives of not only people with diabetes but a variety of other health concerns.
> *Mary Tyler Moore Interview by Chet Cooper*
> *Continued Ability Magazine*

Dixie Carter:
"Certainly if we hope do enhance and extend whatever natural assets we were given, we must expect to make an effort, if not actually great labor."

"I will not do humor that is derived from private parts or going to the bathroom. I won't do anything that involves making fun of people."

Sally Field:
"But there isn't any second half of myself waiting to plug in and make me whole. It's there. I'm already whole."

"I can't deny the fact that you like me! You like me!"

"I was raised to sense what someone wanted me to be and be that kind of person. It took me a long time not to judge myself through someone else's eyes."

"My real assets have always been acting and just being pleasant."

Dr. Leonard McCoy (*Star Trek*)
"A staunchly humane and passionate man, Bones had an acerbic attitude and stood up for principles in the face of skepticism from his colleagues. He frequently clashed with Spock, whom he regarded as infuriatingly cold and implacable." *Dr. Leonard McCoy - Star Trek bbc.co.uk*
"By golly, Jim, I'm beginning to think I can cure a rainy day!"
"I'm a doctor, not a psychiatrist." ("The City on the Edge of Forever")
"I'm a doctor, not an engineer!" ("Mirror, Mirror")
"I'm a doctor, not a mechanic." ("The Doomsday Machine")
"I'm a doctor, not an escalator!" ("Friday's Child")

"I'm a doctor, not a magician!" ("Friday's Child")

Another example of a Cargo Ship would be my stepfather, Jim Thompson. He was the kind of man who was always *there* for all of us. He saw himself as a man with big shoulders for us to lean on. He was definitely stable, dependable, hard-working, and there for the long haul. His joy in life was to provide a comfortable and secure life for my mother. He was always there to make sure she was safe and happy. I remember one evening sitting next to the pool at their home in Texas and Jim telling me that my mother was the greatest gift he had ever received in his life, and that he wanted to make her happy and comfortable in every way that he could. I believe he succeeded. The payment he wanted was her happiness and respect and our love. And he had it. He has since died. He is greatly missed. It's hard to fill the void left by a Cargo Ship once you've had one in your life.

In the workplace, you would probably find Cargo Ships in the helping professions. There are times when we all need someone to "carry the load" for us. When we are sick, or depressed, or grieving, being able to reach out to one of these people would be a good solution. They are extremely organized and get great enjoyment from helping others. They prefer to have a job where they follow a familiar routine. Examples would be, psychologists, ministers, social workers, family practice doctors, medical workers, public relations people, or childcare workers.

As friends, Cargo Ships will be the ones who will be there to help you when you need it most; they are capable of getting the job done. An example would be when you are in the process of moving. They will be there with pick-up truck available, quietly and efficiently getting the job done. When treated with respect, these Cargo Ship friends will stick with you throughout their life. If you have a Cargo Ship as a friend, try to remember to not overuse their helpfulness. Cargo Ships have a tremendous need to "do their duty," and can sometimes allow their friends become another "load" that they have to carry.

As romantic partners, Cargo Ships are stable, dependable, and there for the long haul. They may be a little more deliberate and less exciting than some other choices, but they will provide a comfortable and secure life for you. As stated earlier, they are also caretakers, so they can be counted on to be there in times of need; they will stand by you and see that you are safe. What they want from their partner in return is loyalty, respect, and approval. They are interested in taking care of the day-to-day needs, security, and a peaceful, harmonious home.

What a Cargo Ship needs from you:

- Appreciate how hard they work to make life comfortable for you.

- Try not disturb their routines.

- Respect their need for order and structure.

- Respect their feelings.

- Listen to them when they need to talk.

- Try to stick to established plans.

- Point out to them when they are overwhelming themsevles.

- Show them that they're needed and appreciated.

If you have a Cargo Ship as a partner, you will notice when they become overwhelmed because they will begin to criticize themselves to an excessive degree and withdraw from groups and activities with friends. As it progresses, they may start to over-analyze the problem and start consulting various outside experts for their opinions. As their partner, what you can do to help the Cargo Ship is to encourage them to stop and take care of themselves, even volunteering to take over some of their responsibilities so that they can.

If you are a Cargo Ship and notice you are becoming overwhelmed, here's what you can do to help yourself:

- Talk to a neutral third party about your concerns.

- Begin a regiment of self-care—eating properly, exercise, meditation.

- Begin a new activity or develop a new hobby.

- Look deeper into the situation to see if you might have decided or judged too quickly.

- Allow yourself to step out of your "comfort zone" and try something new.

Exercises that may be helpful:

Look for areas in your life where you have tended to over-commit yourself. Why did you take on additional commitments when you were already fully committed to other things?

Look at areas in your life where you have not followed what you wish you had done; dreams you have accomplished. Are there still some of those dreams you can renew today? Or are there new ones you can discover?

During a crisis, Cargo Ships needs someone to step in and take over some of their responsibilities so that they can take some time for themselves. Some need to get active and take walks, while others need to find someone to talk to. During extreme stress, they need to learn how to go inside and look at their thoughts and not just their feelings.

Cargo Ships search for a Creator who will provide nurturing, support, encouragement, and strength—no matter what situation arises in their lives. They tend to find evidence of spirituality in the day-to-day occurrences that they encounter. They look for a spiritual community that will accept and nurture each person. You may even find a Cargo Ship on the welcoming committee of their spiritual community. As Cargo Ships mature spiritually, they discover a great sense of inner peace and feel comfortable with who they are.

"I am thankful for

> My ability to befriend and care for people
> My warm and enthusiastic manner
> Being in tune with feelings of others and knowing what is important in my life
> The way I invite others in so we can all join in serving the common good

In the storms of life, I can find shelter by

> Finding space and quiet time to reflect on facts of the situation
> Realizing my personal limitations and what is beyond my control
> Assessing what I value, what is most important for my own life, before choosing to serve

To honor myself and my pathway to God, I can

> Develop a few intimate "spiritual friendships" that allow for deep conversations and examination
> Celebrate myself, others, and the beauty in the universe as expressions of the Divine
> Explore what my logical mind can add to my heartfelt pathways"
> *Soul Types*, page 255

ESFJ Prayer: God, please give me patience, and do it *immediately!*

ISFJ Introverted Sensing/Extroverted Feeling

TUGBOAT

A Tugboat's theme is Protector/Guardian/Traditionalist/Nurturer. They thrive on caring for others so that they can reach their goals. Their goal is protecting and caretaking. Their driving force is their ability to be of practical help to others. They are devoted to doing what needs to be done for shelter and safety. Their motto is "Slow and steady wins the race."

I chose a Tugboat to represent these people because tugboats quietly go about their job of helping people throughout their day. They are dependable, get the job done, and are always there to help out. Their whole purpose is to be there for the people they care about and to do it quietly and efficiently. They bring a quiet atmosphere of caring, dependability, and concern to everything that they do.

You can recognize a Tugboat by their gentleness, quietness, and conscientiousness. These people are very private, modest, sensitive, and hardworking. And isn't that what a tugboat does? They are quietly devoted to taking care of the other boats in their home port;

they watch over them and serve them diligently. They have excellent recall of memories, especially about the people they care about. They speak softly and slowly, and dress conservatively.

They are responsible, practical, respectful, dependable, private, unassuming, self-sacrificing people who are always willing to help others. They are especially committed to helping family members and friends reach their goals and potential. In one book (*The Pygmalion Project, Volume II: The Guardian*), Stephen Montgomery describes them as being like beavers, "not simply building and stocking their lodges, but also standing stubborn guard on their ponds afterward, ready to drum out a warning if they spot anything amiss." (25). They resist change, and they want everything to be maintained as it is; as stated earlier, they are the "Guardians of Tradition." Because of this, you will find that they have a difficult time letting go of anything that connects to the past, and you will find that they have a well-maintained area where they keep old mementos.

A Tugboat's view of the world is based on what they see as continuity between what is now and what has been in the past. They do not understand the Intuitive's way of thinking at all, and they have even been heard to say to an Intuitive, "Where in the world do you get your ideas?" They much prefer a predictable, well-thought-out environment, which personifies that need of continuity for them. Indeed, they will stay in awful relationships in order to maintain that continuity. The decision to stay is determined both by their social role (a good parent, employee, spouse) and also by their role as rescuer or nurturer. In fact, Tugboats are often unable to appreciate people who aren't in some way dependent on them.

They also have a quirky sense of humor that they fear that others don't understand or appreciate. This stems from their distinctive and unusual view of reality. In *Personality Type,* Lenore Thompson states that they "keep a running Seinfeld-like commentary in their heads about the absurdities they encounter every day."

Examples of Tugboats in the literature are Jimmy Stewart, Johnny Carson, Jerry Seinfeld, and Tyne Daly.

Jimmy Stewart:
"This was the time of training, when you were learning your craft, and I don't think that you can work too hard at that particular time."

"Never treat your audience as customers, always as partners."

Johnny Carson:
"I know you've been married to the same woman for sixty-nine years. That is marvelous. It must be very inexpensive."

"I was so naive as a kid I used to sneak behind the barn and do nothing."

"Any time four New Yorkers get into a cab together without arguing, a bank robbery has just taken place."

Jerry Seinfeld:
"A bookstore is one of the only pieces of evidence we have that people are still thinking."

"Now they show you how detergents take out bloodstains, a pretty violent image there. I think if you've got a T-shirt with a bloodstain all over it, maybe laundry isn't your biggest problem. Maybe you should get rid of the body before you do the wash."

Tyne Daly:
"I'm interested in playing old ladies because I am becoming one. And I want to become a very good one!"

"I'm sorry I didn't wear paint this morning. I tend not to wear it unless I'm getting highly paid."

"Love is as strict as acting. If you want to love somebody, stand there and do it. If you don't, don't. There are no other choices."

"You know, my hair is very upsetting to people, but it's upsetting on purpose. It is important to look old so that the young will not be afraid of dying. People don't like old women. We don't honor age in our society, and we certainly don't honor it in Hollywood."

"I think Amy's terrific ... She's really interesting to me, but I can't think of any age I'd want to go back to. I don't want to do anything again. For me, backward is not a direction."

"Think about all these different kinds of women. Think about all the different looks we used to be able to see on the screen. Not one of these women was trying to fit a standard. But today you can put any six girls in a row and have a very hard time distinguishing them. Everybody's trying to fit a mold."

"A critic never fights the battle; they just go around shooting the wounded."

I have a friend who is a Tugboat personality. Her name is Melissa. Melissa is dependable, conscientious, and caring. She is the kind of person that you know you can count on to be there when you are going through troubled waters. Whenever I have had a problem, no matter how busy she is, she lays aside whatever she is doing and completely focuses on my problem and me. There are not many people who will do that. She thinks that I don't notice that she does that, but I do. Melissa's family is the most important thing in her life, and I'm sure both her husband and daughter appreciate and benefit greatly from her devotion to them. As mild and easygoing as Melissa is, I would not want to be around if someone threatened to harm either her husband or daughter, though. She stands up for the people she cares about. In the workplace, I know that Melissa can be counted on to do the very best that she can with each family she works with. Her paperwork will be impeccable, and she will give her complete attention to each family she works with. It would be great to have a whole team of Tugboats.

In a career, you will find them in positions where they can help other people reach their goals and even help them develop a plan to reach those goals. Examples would be health care workers, teachers, clergy, designers, counselors, or human services workers. These are the people who are dependable and hardworking. They are good listeners and always ready to help others in practical ways. They are much better at applying information that they attained through direct experience, rather than imagining possibilities that haven't occurred yet.

As a friend, a Tugboat is warm and friendly, but only shares those feelings with one or two close friends. A Tugboat likes to have close friends that they can talk things over with. They like being around other people, but can be a bit reserved around them.

If you are in a relationship with a Tugboat, you will find that the Tugboat notices and is aware of your feelings and needs, and is quick to offer practical assistance. They are very generous, warm, and kind individuals who truly care about others. Family is their main focus and concern. You may find that they will consistently place your needs above their own—even at the risk of not meeting their own personal needs. But, as their partner, you will be the main priority in their life, and their goal will be to make you comfortable and happy. They are also private and do not like conflict, so they will withdraw when provoked or criticized rather than let you know their feelings.

When a Tugboat is in a "bad" relationship, where they are with someone who takes advantage of them, they will stay in the relationship rather than leave. They will place the blame on themselves and continue to do what they can to make their partner happy.

What a Tugboat needs from you:

- Mutual commitment.

- Companionship.

- Listening.

- Time to think about things.

- Appreciation for the things they do for you.

- Appreciation for their practical approach to life.

- Punctuality.

- Understanding of their need to spend time alone.

You will know when your Tugboat is feeling overwhelmed when they become sad and negative about the future, or when they look at the situation and are unable to think about alternatives. Sometimes they even develop health problems because of suppressed anger. What you can do to help them is to stop and listen to their concerns, help them to look at their feelings about what is going on, and if at all possible, go out and make a couple of "life-saving" runs for them to rescue other people. Also, help them see if hidden anger is causing them this problem.

If you are a Tugboat and notice yourself becoming overwhelmed and experiencing some of the above symptoms, here are some things you can do to help yourself:

- Look at the negative situation and think about what good could happen.

- Discuss the situation with friends and let them help you to look at the "bigger picture." (Seeing the bigger picture is something that a Tugboat needs help in doing, because they are too focused on the details of their day-to-day caretaking duties.

- Find a creative outlet to occupy your mind, one where there is no pressure for things to turn out a particular way.

- Learn to say "No."

Exercises that may be helpful:

Make a list of the things that excite you (Oriah Mountain Dreamer says "What do you yearn for?") What kind of person would you be if you could? What can you do to take steps toward becoming that person? Today? This week? A quote from Victor Hugo: "It is nothing to die; it is frightening not to live." How do you feel about this statement? Can you apply it to your life?

Learn to recognize what *you* want in a situation. You have a tendency to be so focused on taking care of those you love and those around you that you forget to take care of yourself and meet your own needs. Allow yourself to say "no" occasionally. Even allow yourself to feel anger—sometimes it is anger that allows you to say "no." When you hide your anger, you allow resentment to build and may find that you begin to exhibit physical symptoms.

When a Tugboat experiences a crisis, they need friends and family to help pull them out of their caretaking role and to teach them how to look at the bigger picture. They can begin by becoming involved in creative projects such as art, woodworking, or dance, where there is no pressure for any specific result. This is a time when getting in touch with that Intuitive side of themselves (that they dismissed previously) can help them take the next step in their growth. During these times, they need to *not* be needed. They need to be allowed to take care of themselves and to give that time to themselves that they have so freely given to others all of their lives.

For Tugboats, doing good deeds, helping others, and taking care of their families are the things that bring them to a spiritual understanding. They like to belong to a spirituality community where there is clear structure, traditions, and loyalty, and where they know what to expect. As the spirituality of the Tugboat matures, they are finally able to see the interconnectedness of all things, to accept that the good and the bad, the pleasure and pain, the sadness and joy are all linked. And when they can take that next step into seeing that they, too, are worthy of being nurtured, then they become the whole and complete people they were meant to be.

"I am thankful for

My understanding of what matters most
My friendly, warm, people-oriented style
My gifts of communication and creativity, which allow me to advance human aspirations

In the storms of life, I can find shelter by

Pulling inward and considering all the hopeful possibilities
Assessing what is most important and finding personal confirmation for my values system
Being direct with others about my views, letting them know where I stand

To honor myself and my pathway to God, I can

Gather with kindred spirits for inspiration and understanding
Champion efforts to create the atmosphere for nurturing human potential I can so clearly envision
Determine the logical underpinnings of my values and beliefs in order to confirm what my heart already knows"
Soul Types, page 270

ISFJ Prayer: God, help me to be more laid-back and relaxed, and help me to do it *exactly* right.

Section 5
NFs—Idealists

Idealists are the people who are focused on the big picture and on the characteristics that bring people together, not on the things that separate them. These are the people who are passionate about the things they are interested in and are very imaginative and creative in their outlook and approach to solving problems. They do not like to follow the rules; in fact, they are pretty much non-conformists, and march to the beat of their own drummer. At the same time, they very closely live by their own "ethical" rules and values, which mainly consist of not violating or injuring another person. They have a very strong conscience and a very strong aversion toward cruelty or exploitation of others. Their drive is to show compassion and goodwill to everyone, even their enemies. They have a strong distaste for conflict and base their self-esteem on their ability to maintain good feelings toward other people. This innate characteristic keeps them filled with good intentions and a positive approach to all people, which is one of the reasons why animosity or conflict of any kind is completely abhorrent to them. This means they have a tendency to repress their own angry or negative feelings because to acknowledge those feelings would damage their own self-concept.

Being an "Idealist" myself, I have found that in situations where others believe I should be at odds with someone because of their behavior towards me, I will make every effort to find common ground—something that will bring us together. I even feel that if someone is to be hurt or come out at a disadvantage in a situation, it should be me. This is not just martyrdom, but a way of preserving my own internal ideals about not hurting anyone else—in other words, a way of preserving my own integrity in a negative situation.

Idealists are future-oriented and prefer to focus on "what could be" rather than on "what is"—they tend to focus on the potential in a situation rather than on the actuality of it. They have strong passions and excitement from within themselves for the causes that interest them. Indeed, in this aspect, I find that I sometimes lose track of obstacles or barriers in a situation because they don't fit in with the vision I have of what I want to happen. And I can sometimes become so passionate and excited about a project that I am working on that I don't realize that others may not share that passion and enthusiasm.

Idealists have a unique characteristic in their search for the "Self." The "self" is seen as an important aspect of a person, an important inner core, a deeply intrinsic part of a person's being that the other temperaments do not fully understand. They seek not only to comprehend and get in touch with their own inner self, but also to help others find theirs. This inner Self is experienced as something that is constantly evolving and leading us on to our greatest potential.

And they are extreme romantics. This, fortunately and unfortunately, is very true. They look for the ideal "soul mate." It is a search for someone with whom they can share their passionate inner selves, and be accepted and understood. Believe me, it is not an easy search, because, as likely as not, we push people away with our intensity of feeling once they realize it is there.

I found it interesting to learn that there has never been an Idealist American president, as stated in *Presidential Temperament* by Ray Choiniere and David Kiersey. They say:

There have been no Idealist Presidents. Why this is so is open to many explanations, of which the most likely concerns the matter of power. The political arena is above all a place of power, and Idealists find the pursuit of power inimical to what they see as their mission in life: personal fulfillment and the fulfillment of persons. When they see power they do not covet it, when they have the opportunity they do not seek it, when it is offered them, they will not accept it. (493)

I do believe this is true; Idealists do not seek or want power. I also believe that in the American political system, the political seeker must sell out some of their ideals in order to receive the support from the various factions that support the system. An Idealist will not sell out his ideals, his values, or his beliefs, and most certainly not for power, which is something they don't want anyway. They can support their ideals much better from outside the presidential political system.

The Idealists are:

ENFJ—Cabin Cruiser

INFJ—Submarine

ENFP—Catamaran

INFP—Nautilus

ENFJ   Extroverted Feeling/Introverted Intuition

CABIN CRUISERS

The theme of a Cabin Cruiser is Envisioner/Teacher/Sage/Giver. They thrive on being catalysts that draw out the best in others. Their themes are mentoring, leading people to their potential, and influencing others to learn and grow. Their driving force is to be truly helpful and to bring harmony into the lives of others. Their motto is, "One person *can* make a difference."

I chose a Cabin Cruiser to represent this style because a cabin cruiser is an all-around boat. They are used for play and entertaining, but are also able to do their share of the work. These people, and boats, are very adaptable and are useful for many occasions. They are very patient and conscientious.

Cabin Cruisers are identified by their playful and entertaining qualities. They want to ensure that everyone has a good time and is at ease. They like to travel and have fun in style. But don't be deceived;

they are quite capable of working when the need arises. They can be hard on themselves as they try to live up to their own ideal of what they believe they should accomplish. They also have an immense desire to be helpful to others and have a built-in radar system that keeps them alert for other boaters who need rescuing.

Cabin Cruisers are often the humanitarians we meet in our lives, the mentors who work to help others reach their potential. They are intuitive in their approach to the people they meet, and are often able to draw out their hidden talents and gifts.

They have a gift, or curse, of being able to see both sides of a disagreement. This can get them into trouble because, since they can understand both sides of an issue, they can have a difficult time making a stand themselves, or making a choice of which side to go with. Approval and recognition are important to them, but they have a difficult time allowing others to know who they really are.

An example of a Cabin Cruiser, the "all-around" person, would be Michael Jordan. He likes to be out and about, enjoys himself, is outgoing, but is also reliable and dependable. He exemplifies security, ability, and pleasure in living. You can just see that he enjoys whatever it is he is doing.

> "I've always believed that if you put in the work, the results will come. I don't do things half-heartedly. Because I know if I do, then I can expect half-hearted results."

> "Just play. Have fun. Enjoy the game."

> "The game is my life. It demands loyalty and responsibility, and it gives me back fulfillment and peace."

Other examples listed in the literature are Oprah Winfrey, Diane Sawyer, Dick Van Dyke, and John Denver.

Oprah Winfrey:
"For every one of us that succeeds, it's because there's somebody there to show you the way out. The light doesn't always necessarily have to be in your family; for me, it was teachers and school."

"I am a woman in process. I'm just trying like everybody else. I try to take every conflict, every experience, and learn from it. Life is never dull."

"I believe that every single event in life that happens is an opportunity to choose love over fear."

"I don't think you ever stop giving. I really don't. I think it's an ongoing process. And it's not just about being able to write a check. It's being able to touch somebody's life."

"My philosophy is that not only are you responsible for your life, but doing the best at this moment puts you in the best place for the next moment."

"The more you praise and celebrate your life, the more there is in life to celebrate."

"Where there is no struggle, there is no strength."

"You are what you are by what you believe!"

"You know you are on the road to success if you would do your job and not be paid for it."

Diane Sawyer:
"I'm always fascinated by the way memory diffuses fact."

"The one lesson I have learned is that there is no substitute for paying attention."

"Of all of the forces that make for a better world, none is so indispensable, none so powerful, as hope."

"It's in the preparation—in those dreary pedestrian virtues they taught you in seventh grade and you didn't believe. It's making the extra call and caring a lot."

Dick Van Dyke
"Women will never be as successful as men because they have no wives to advise them."

John Denver
"He regularly did benefits and donated his time and money—but his motivation was because of the empathy he felt with the people who requested his time. He believed that their commitment was honorable, and he didn't want to let them down."
Personality Type - pg. 359

"I believe that we are here for each other, not against each other. Everything comes from an understanding that you are a gift in my life—whoever you are, whatever our differences."

"I would so much like young people to have a sense of the gift that they are. Not many of them feel like that."

"Perhaps love is like a resting place, / a shelter from the storm. / It exists to give you comfort. / It is there to keep you warm. / And in those times of trouble, / when you are most alone, / the memory of love will bring you home."

"I would make my job a work of art. I would like whatever it is that I'm doing—everyone's experience of me, everyone's interaction with me, everyone's discussion, conversation, relationship with me—[to be] an event within which they get to see who they are. I would make of my life a work of art."

A personal example that I know who is a Cabin Cruiser is Judy. Judy works with retired seniors, helping them to find purpose in their lives by helping other seniors who need help. What a wonderful career for a Cabin Cruiser! She is helping two groups of people at the same time. The volunteers who come to her find meaning and purpose in their lives by learning to help other people.

In the business world, you will find that a Cabin Cruiser can entertain their clients in style and ensure that everyone is enjoying themselves. They are willing to go anywhere in order to entertain. They can get the job done *and* entertain at the same time. They have an innate ability to enrich the lives of other people; they can help other people understand themselves more clearly. They are also extremely good at organizing people and are attracted to careers that help them bring out the best in others. They have a strong interest in improving the careers that determine human relationships. They are usually good writers and editors. They enjoy helping other people make decisions which change their lives for the better.

Good career choices for Cabin Cruisers are therapist, teacher, school psychologist, child care worker, magazine editor, corporate trainer, fundraiser, writer/journalist, social worker, career counselor.

As a friend, a Cabin Cruiser is happy to take you along wherever they go. The more the merrier. They like to party, but are also stable and sheltering during the turbulent times of your life. People tend to love Cabin Cruisers. They are fun to be with; they truly understand and love people; they are honest and have the ability to do many different things. It is difficult to find them at home, though, because they prefer to be on the move and will usually have something going on.

A relationship with a Cabin Cruiser can be a romp through the days of your life. This type of person is an "all-around" person. They like to be out and about, but they are also reliable. Marriage to a Cabin

Cruiser can almost seem idyllic at times if you like festivity and travel in your life. If you are a stay-at-home person, your patience will be tried to the limit. Knowing yourself and recognizing the qualities of your partner can be beneficial and rewarding.

Harmony is important to a Cabin Cruiser, and they will go to unusual lengths to understand their partners and make them happy. In the process, they often put their partner's needs ahead of their own. They can get trapped in a position where they are always the person who takes care of others, so that they are not truly sharing relationships— and in the process, they aren't sharing their true selves with anyone. What they really need from their partner is for the partner to get to really know them, to listen to them.

What a Cabin Cruiser needs from others:

- Encourage them to express their feeling and opinions.

- Share yourself openly with them.

- Help them to take care of their own needs too.

- Recognize and appreciate the many things they do for you.

You will be aware when the Cabin Cruiser is becoming overwhelmed because they will become openly hostile to others—or they may go the other direction, becoming obsessed with trying to make others get along. Uncharacteristic angry feelings can surface, creating waves which rock their boat in ever-increasing intensity. You can help them by helping them to look at all of the things they have done and accomplished, the contributions they have made. Help them recognize and appreciate the things they did to try to make things turn out well. Show that you, too, recognize and appreciate their contributions.

If you are a Cabin Cruiser and notice yourself beginning to have problems, here are some things you can do:

- Talk through the situation with a neutral third party.

- Try a change in schedule or routine.

- Understand that your feelings are as important as the other person's feelings.

- Don't be afraid to have an opinion.

- Don't forsake your own needs for others' all of the time. Take the time to take care of you.

- Ask for the feedback you need from others.

Exercises that may be helpful:

Learn to pay attention to your body—to notice when you need to rest. Take time to care for yourself, the way you would care for someone you love. Learn to ask people not only what they need from you, but what they don't need from you, because sometimes you want to help others more than they want help.

In times of a crisis, a Cabin Cruiser needs someone to step in and take care of all the people they are helping. They need to be able to spend time alone, to learn to search inside themselves and find the truth of who they are and why they do what they do. Once they find this internal connection, they will never again *not* take time for themselves.

Spiritually, Cabin Cruisers develop a belief that is people-centered. They see worth and dignity in all people and try to help each person see their own worth and significance. They seek out communities and groups that are nurturing, warm, and supportive. Since they are so good at organization, they will be involved in arranging retreats, programs, and study groups that will meet the needs of other members in the group. As they grow spiritually, Cabin Cruisers will recognize the love in each person they meet, allowing the love that is there between people to guide them.

"I am thankful for

My understanding of what matters most
My friendly, warm, people-centered style
My gifts of communication and creativity, which allow me to advance human aspirations
My passion for helping others become whole

In the storms of life, I can find shelter by

Pulling inward and considering all hopeful possibilities
Assessing what is most important and finding personal confirmation for my values system
Being direct with others about my views, letting them know where I stand

To honor myself and my pathway to God, I can

Gather with kindred spirits for inspiration and understanding
Champion efforts to create the atmospheres for nurturing human potential I can so clearly envision
Determine the logical underpinnings of my values and beliefs in order to confirm what my heart already knows"
Soul Types, page 270

ENFJ Prayer: God, help me to help others today and to trust in your guidance. But do you mind putting that in writing?

INFJ Introverted Intuition/Extroverted Feeling

SUBMARINE

A Submarine's theme is Forseer/Observer/Protector/Empath. They thrive on helping others. They focus on people's hidden motives by patiently observing what they do and listening intently. Their driving force is their own internal world of what is possible, and they are truly excited about developing new ideas and activities. Their theme is foresight. Their motto is, "I'll find a way!"

I used a Submarine to represent this personality because they tend to keep their insights and feelings hidden, presenting a very different picture to the world. They are private, but work quietly toward their long-term goals. They like to work behind the scenes, staying hidden and calm. In their inner world they observe much and create possibilities of all that they observe, especially for other people. Because of this very acute observation and connection to other people, they are often seen as being "psychic." Many times they do develop a deep connection to spirituality.

It is sometimes difficult to recognize a Submarine because they are, by definition, secretive and cautious. They keep their true nature hidden from their acquaintances. They keep a low profile, or at least, a hidden profile. By that, I mean they present to the public one type of exterior, but they keep their true character hidden. They are very thoughtful, creative, and even mysterious.

Submarines use unconventional paths to get to where they want to go. They trust their own visions, are intense, reserved, patient and can quietly exert their influence in subtle ways. They are creative, observers, private, easily offended, guarded, sad, and perfectionistic.

The best example that comes to mind when I think of a Submarine personality is the character portrayed by Clint Eastwood in the *A Fistful of Dollars* movies. The character he portrayed in those movies was definitely secretive, kept to himself, and did not let anyone know who he really was—in fact he was called the "Man With No Name." He was an enigma. As I watched these movies, I was intrigued with the separateness and the hidden aspects of his character. Everyone knew that we would never *know* this man, that he would never share himself openly with anyone. I found his character to be fascinating. Because as unapproachable as he seemed, the things he did were because of his strong values toward not seeing innocent people taken advantage of.

> "I don't think it's nice, you laughin'. You see, my mule don't like people laughing. He gets the crazy idea you're laughin' at him. Now if you apologize, like I know you're going to, I might convince him that you really didn't mean it."

> "As the lean, cold-eyed, cobra-quick gunfighter—the laconic 'Man With No Name'—Clint became the first of the 'anti-heroes.' The cynical, enigmatic loner with a clouded past is the same character Eastwood fans have been savouring ever since"
> *A Fistful of Dollars - Video Case Cover Information*

Another example of a Submarine would be Batman. The whole idea behind Batman (or Superman) is that no one knows who he is. He is Bruce Wayne. But behind the facade of Bruce Wayne lies another, hidden and secretive persona of which others are unaware. Bruce Wayne is very kind, warm, caring, and has a very creative approach to his dreams and goals. He also has strong values, and he cares deeply for other people.

In the literature, Submarines listed are Shirley MacLaine, Michael Landon, Carrie Fisher, Nelson Mandela.

Shirley MacLaine:
At the end of her pilgrimage of walking the Camino, Shirley MacLaine says in her book *The Camino*, "I couldn't share my experience with Anna. It was too soon. I have communicated with her since the trek and explained that I needed to write what happened to me rather than talk."

"I can't get MacLaine to change. Shirley MacLaine is extremely perceptive and follows her own vision."
The Camino, by Shirley MacLaine pgs. 217-218

Michael Landon:
"Somebody ought to tell us, right at the start of our lives, that we are dying. Then we might live life to the limit every minute of every day. Do it, I say, whatever you want to do, do it now."
Carol (Channah Leah) Shoemaker
TJones2020@aol.com

"He was an immensely talented man; a man with a mission. Maybe his shows even helped to 'repair some broken hearts and some broken promises'—what we in Judaism call *Tikkun Olam* (repairing the world)."
(Carol (Channah Leah) Shoemaker)
Conversations with Michael Landon
by Tom Ito(1992)

"Dreaming is one thing, and working towards the dream is one thing, but working with expectations in mind, I think, is very self-defeating."

"Do it! I say. Whatever you want to do, do it now! There are only so many tomorrows."

Carrie Fisher:
"I think of my body as a side effect of my mind."

"Instant gratification takes too long."

"You can't find any true closeness in Hollywood, because everybody does the fake closeness so well."

Nelson Mandela:
"As we are liberated from our own fear, our presence automatically liberates others."

"For to be free is not merely to cast off one's chains, but to live in a way that respects and enhances the freedom of others."

"I learned that courage was not the absence of fear, but the triumph over it. The brave man is not he who does not feel afraid, but he who conquers that fear."

"If there are dreams about a beautiful South Africa, there are also roads that lead to their goal. Two of these roads could be named Goodness and Forgiveness."

"If you talk to a man in a language he understands, that goes to his head. If you talk to him in his language, that goes to his heart."

"If you want to make peace with your enemy, you have to work with your enemy. Then he becomes your partner."

"There is no easy walk to freedom anywhere, and many of us will have to pass through the valley of the shadow of death again and again before we reach the mountaintop of our desires."

"There is nothing like returning to a place that remains unchanged to find the ways in which you yourself have altered."

"We must use time wisely and forever realize that the time is always ripe to do right."

In the work world, a Submarine would be useful as an "undercover" type of person. Some businesses use corporate spies to scope out the competition. Submarines would be ideal in this type of job.

In a friendship, you may be unaware that you are dealing with a Submarine unless a necessity arises and they need to show you this different aspect of themselves. Their very purpose is to keep their true nature secret. You will see only what they choose to show you; the biggest part of their character is beneath the surface. They are extremely insightful and see things that are not obvious to others. They have a strong sense of "knowing."

Submarines are attracted to careers where they can do what they feel is right. They want to be able to live their lives in such a way that they are true to their deeply-held principles. They are often found as clergy, teachers, doctors, psychologists, psychiatrists, musicians, or philosophers.

If you are friends with a Submarine, you will already know that they place their values as a measuring stick with which to accept people into their lives. They have no time for people of low morals, or whose values do not coincide with their own. They like to have a few close friends. They are surprised to find that many people are drawn to them. But they are very warm, caring people who look at things in novel and unusual ways, and they love to inspire their friends to reach for higher goals.

Even when you have an intimate relationship with a Submarine, you may never know the "below the surface" nature of this person. Sometimes you may glimpse that there is something else there, but most of the time, you only get to interact with the surface person. They are excellent listeners and come up with original and creative insights that will help you see things in a different way. But they do like to stay behind the scenes and not call attention to themselves. They love to show their affection and want you to reciprocate with affirmations of your own.

What a Submarine needs from you:

- Respect their values.

- Give them time to explore their passions and interests in depth.

- Appreciate their novel and creative ideas.

- Encourage them to make their dreams come true.

- Respect their strong feelings about things.

- Listen to their hunches and insights.

If you are in a relationship with a Submarine and you notice them becoming unusually negative, or spending time in "mindless" pursuits such as watching television or playing endless games of solitaire, you will know that they are feeling overwhelmed. You can help them best by diverting their attention from the situation and focusing on something that is more healthy and positive. Of course, if you are in a relationship with Batman, it might be best if you just prepared his bat suit and had it ready for him.

If you are a Submarine and notice yourself becoming overwhelmed, here are some things you may want to do to help yourself:

- Take time to exercise, or enjoy a physical activity that you like to do.

- List the facts and details of a situation instead of trying to figure out what it means.

- If you are becoming angry, walk away and calm down.

- Don't allow yourself to become obsessed with the details; stop and look at your main goal.

- Learn how to relax.

Exercises that may be helpful:

Notice when and how you withdraw from people and make yourself an outsider when you could be part of the activity. Observe your self-talk at these times. What are you saying to yourself about the situation?

Pay attention to the "feelings" you get about other people. Do you find these feelings to be helpful to you, or for the other person?

In times of crisis, a Submarine need the support of being with other people. They also need to see the impact and effect they have on other people. I have even read the suggestion that a Submarine could make a list of the love they have received from other people, a list of the love they have given, and another list of the times they have hurt those who love them. This is not meant as a guilt exercise, but as a way to get in touch with their feelings on a deeper level.

Spirituality comes easily to Submarines because they are already in close contact with their intuition and hidden visions. Many Submarines will study different spiritual practices in depth, but they need to take the time to develop their own understanding and way of believing in a higher power. Their intuition will guide them to their inner wisdom, and they will clearly know what path they need to follow. As they mature spiritually, Submarines will become more in touch with their hearts and will transform not only themselves, but others as well.

"I am thankful for

My creativity, which allows me to envision different solutions
My optimism in trying circumstances
My ability to help people recognize their potential
The way I communicate to others

In the storms of life, I can find shelter by

Realizing that it is okay to seek help
Finding a listening ear so that I can discern feelings
Assessing the details and tasks, giving away what I cannot handle

To honor myself and my pathway to God, I can

Find creative ways to engage my imagination
Create space for myself to be alone with my thoughts, prayers, or musings
Notice the spiritual in the details of creation"
Soul Types, page 165

INFJ Prayer: Lord, help me not be a perfectionist. (Did I spell that correctly?)

ENFP Extroverted Intuition/Introverted Feeling

POWER CATAMARAN

The theme of a Power Catamaran is Champion/Visionary/Inspirer/ Advocate. They are unconventional, energetic, friendly, curious, and seldom impressed with rules or what they "should" do. Their goal is to encourage and inspire others to use their potential. Their driving force is the outer world of possibilities. Their motto could be "There is always a better way…"

I had to look at a lot of boats to find one that could represent a Visionary/Inspirer/Champion. I finally found the Ellips and knew I had found my match. It is outgoing, novel, on the cutting edge, carefree, exuberant, and decidedly unconventional. Can't you just see the passion in these boats? This is a boat that loves life, loves being creative, and does it full-out in its own unique style.

Picture of Ellips Catamaran courtesy of Paritet Boat

You can spot Power Catamarans by noticing their off-beat energy, their fun and loving imagination, and their eager ability to inspire and motivate others. These people have lots of charisma, love people and crowds, are attracted to the unusual and the unconventional, and are easily talked into doing "wild and crazy" things. They are hyper-alert to what is going on around them and so are very perceptive and adaptable.

Power Catamarans live in the realm of possibilities, and when they are interested in their latest project, they can think of little else; they become obsessed. They see a problem not as a barrier but a challenge, a puzzle to be overcome. And they are tenacious in their quest to overcome that challenge.

They are quick to grasp the significance of an event and are curious and interested in everything ... as long as it is genuine. They do not like "phoniness" or dishonesty in people. They have a great concern for others and are always available to their friends. They are intuitive about understanding and connecting to other people. They are extremely open, honest, and accepting of others. They are often charismatic because of their high energy, their love of others, their ability to give of themselves, and their natural "high" from the love of living—not to mention their unique slant on life.

Examples of Catamarans are Andy Rooney, Paul Harvey, Carol Burnett, Martin Short, Meg Ryan, Sandra Bullock, and the fictional character Ariel from *The Little Mermaid*. Just by looking at this list, can you see how each one of them represents their own unique, outgoing style? They are all exceptional in their fields because of their uniqueness, their warmth, their love of people, their sensitivities, and their creativity.

Andy Rooney:
"Andy Rooney is known to millions for his wry, humorous, and sometimes controversial essays that have been the signature end piece of *60 Minutes* for decades.

The 2004-05 season marks Rooney's twenty-seventh doing these unique reports, 'A Few Minutes with Andy Rooney'" (CBS).
"A Few Minutes with Andy Rooney," CBS

135

Andy Rooney Quotes:

"Computers make it easier to do a lot of things, but most of the things they make it easier to do don't need to be done. Making duplicate copies and computer printouts of things no one wanted even one of in the first place is giving America a new sense of purpose."

Paul Harvey:

"Paul Harvey is both a newscaster and a storyteller beloved across the nation. His broadcasts emphasize the viewpoints of 'the heart of America'—the millions who still cherish the personal qualities of those who have made this country great. From that point of view, Paul will frequently make emphatic comment on events both at home and abroad. Perhaps the one word most often used to describe Paul Harvey's broadcasts is 'courageous.' He has also been referred to as 'the burr under the saddle of the American conscience.'"

KLMJ-FM Paul Harvey Advertisement

Paul Harvey Quotes:

"Golf is a game in which you yell 'fore,' shoot six, and write down five."

"Like what you do. If you don't like it, do something else."

Carol Burnett Quotes:

"Celebrity was a long time in coming; it will go away. Everything goes away."

"Giving birth is like taking your lower lip and forcing it over your head."

"I don't have false teeth. Do you think I'd buy teeth like these?"

"I have always grown from my problems and challenges, from the things that don't work out; that's when I've really learned."

"I liked myself better when I wasn't me."

"This is to explain just how your mom turned out to be the kind of hairpin she is."

"When you have a dream, you've got to grab it and never let go."

Martin Short Quotes:
"What's great about being a character actor is you know that you can survive forever. It's not about the gloss of your eyebrows."

Meg Ryan Quotes:
"Fame is also a test of character at times... Sometimes I pass the test; sometimes I'm a pain in the ass. Sometimes I'm like, 'Oh, God! I just want to buy some tampons!'"

"People are always telling me that change is good. But all that means is something you didn't want to happen has happened."

Sandra Bullock:
"Sandra's personality is just overwhelming. I've never seen her in a bad mood. She really goes out of her way to make everyone happy" (Chris O'Donnell).

Sandra Bullock Quotes:
"This past year has been an evolution for me, in terms of knowing what you're made of and being challenged enough. A lot of things in life get thrown at you and you go, Wow, that's painful. But then you go, Oh, *that's* why it happened."

"Y'know, I always think I know everything, then somebody shows me that I don't and I'm like, Wow, that's a shocker. So I'm just trying to enjoy it all. I feel like a huge sponge—I just want to experience everything. Do I really live my life? Am I really enjoying every single second? I'm trying to make sure I do that."

"Beginnings are usually scary and endings are usually sad, but it's the middle that counts. You have to remember this when you find yourself at the beginning."

"The key to any good relationship, on-screen and off, is communication, respect, and I guess you have to like the way the other person smells—and he smelled real nice."

"I have an expensive hobby: buying homes, redoing them, tearing them down and building them up the way they want to be built. I want to be an architect."

"I didn't know Bacardi should be mixed with anything, so I just drank it straight. My mom took me to hospital because she thought I'd taken drugs."

Ariel from *The Little Mermaid* (Disney Movie)
Look at this stuff, isn't it neat? / Wouldn't ya think my collection's complete / Wouldn't you think I'm the girl / Girl who has everything / Look at this trove, treasures untold / How many wonders can one cavern hold? / Looking around you'd think / Sure, she's got everything / I've got gadjets and gizmos aplenty / I have whoozits and whatzis galore / You want thingamabobs? I've got twenty / But who cares? No big deal / I want more.

I don't know when/I don't know how/But I know something's starting right now/Watch and you'll see/Some day I'll be/Part of your world.

"I'm sixteen years old! I'm not a child anymore!"

Up where they walk, up where they run, up where they stay all day in the sun. Wandering free...Wish I could...Part of that world.
-Ariel

My daughter Sarah is a Catamaran, and I can vouch for the fact that Catamarans are not your routine children. She was extremely independent and creative at a very early age, being very determined to do things *her* way. She would fixate on something, and nothing anyone could do would change her mind. She loved being with lots of friends and was hardly ever alone, inventing creative ways to entertain them. To give you an example of her obsessiveness, she owned over three hundred My Little Ponies, and I believe she created at least fifteen different ways of playing with them: hide the pony, name the ponies, throwing the ponies, etc., besides the "normal" recommended ways. She didn't talk; she neighed. I think she truly believed she *was* a horse.

Now that she is older—in her 20s—she is still the unconventional one. She currently has her hair cut in a Mohawk and drives an older Bronco that is about four feet off the ground. She is outgoing, exuberant, "artsy," creative, and extremely loving. Her energy and love of life are amazing and contagious. And she can always find a four-leaf-clover within minutes, wherever she is!

In the workplace, these people stand out. They are very bright and capable and genuinely interested in people. Catamarans are extremely innovative and are definitely not your routine workers. They possess many skills—in fact, an unusually broad range of skills—and will do well in any area that interests them. They are at their best when they can be creative and intuitive and work closely with people.

A Catamaran needs to feel that they are living their lives as their "real" self, and everything they do must be consistent with their values. Jobs that consist of lots of details will quickly grow old; they need to be busy, creative, flexible, and independent. When you look at the picture of the Ellips, can't you just feel the excitement, the fun, the uniqueness? It is outgoing, innovative, functional, diverse, with many ways of looking at the outside world. Recommended careers are psychologist, consultant, actor/actress, politician, diplomat, writer/ journalist, television reporter, songwriter, musician, filmmaker, bartender, poet, radio broadcaster.

As friends, Catamarans are very social and outgoing. They tend to be very much in tune with other people's feelings and perspectives. Just watch an Ellips and you will see that they are energetic and fun. They are especially drawn to other Intuitive and Feeling types, and to other Extraverts who are enthusiastic about life. They will have friends from all areas of life because they have the ability to relate to all types of people easily. If you have a friend who is an Ellips, you will truly enjoy being around them. They will make you feel special and will find ways of bringing out the best in you. When you are depressed or down, they will lift your spirits and see the bright side of things. If you own boat is temporarily marooned, they will be the ones who will buzz in and take you for an exhilarating spin in their own unique fashion.

In relationships, Catamarans are fun. They make you feel special and find creative ways to show you how important you are to them. Because they are so enthusiastic and aware of other people's feelings, they will be the ones who will notice when you've had a bad day and find a unique way to make it up to you—in fact, they will see cheering you up as their responsibility.

There are a couple of areas where they can have problems, though. One potential problem area is that if there are problems in a relationship, they see the problems as their fault. They may even stay in a "bad" relationship long after they should have left.

What a Catamaran needs from you:

- Don't bother them about being messy.

- Appreciate their creativity, curiosity, and uniqueness.

- Be patient when they need to process things privately.

- Understand their need to try new and novel things.

- Tell them how much you care about them.

- Encourage them to keep growing and experimenting with life.

- Understand their need to put some thing off until later.

If you are in a relationship with a Catamaran and you notice that they are becoming depressed, are obsessing, are overly concerned about health issues, or are starting to get frustrated with the details that they usually don't even pay attention to, then you know they are becoming stressed and overwhelmed. What you can do to help is to encourage them to take time for themselves—to get away and relax. Quiet meditation, or just contemplative thinking, can be helpful. If they are into a reflective art style like painting, writing, or music, help them to take time to use their internal ability to draw these things out. Sometimes massage, exercise, or even a relaxing bubble bath can do wonders.

If you are a Catamaran and find yourself running around in circles, beating yourself to death with your own waves, here are some things you can do for yourself that will help:

- Make the space to attend to your physical needs—for example, exercise, massage, healthy food, meditation, or aromatherapy.

- Learn to say "no" to your friends and family. Set limits and boundaries.

- Make periodic checks to make sure you are still navigating on course toward your goals; maintain a sense of direction.

- Spend time alone once in awhile to internally visit your purpose and sense of being "you."

- Don't bottle up anger inside. Stop and look at what is upsetting you so that you can express it in an effective manner.

- Look at how you truly feel about things.

- Allow yourself to develop your skills; because you have so many interests and can do so many things, you don't always take the time to truly develop your skills.

- Take care of your own needs too. We know you like to take care of others, but you must take of yourself first.

- Keep a positive attitude.

Exercises that may be helpful:

Have a one-on-one talk with a friend that you feel you may have hurt during a stressful time. Really listen to what they have to say. Then calmly be open with them about any issues that you may still have.

Notice how you tend to dismiss the present moment because of anticipating something in the future. Are you becoming obsessed with a particular person or idea? When you stop and look at the present, can you discover something that you were overlooking by thinking about the future, or an obsessing thought?

During times of crisis, Power Catamarans need time for quietness and rest. They go full speed so much of their lives that a crisis can deplete them. Personal rituals that have meaning to them should be observed—and they will have some that are important to them. Crisis is a time for them to get in touch with their inner selves, their inner creativity, through such methods as writing poetry, painting, yoga, music, or experiencing a healing massage.

Spirituality for a Catamaran is very personal. They are extremely curious and may search out the philosophies of many different spiritualities before settling on one that feels right to them. They tend to be exuberant toward their spirituality and will encourage others to experience the same peace, love, and joy that they have found. Finding a group with similar beliefs is very important to the Catamaran. Techniques that a Catamaran may use in their spiritual practice are music, poetry, journaling, art, drama, dance, helping others, yoga, tai chi, meditation, and guided imagery. As a Catamaran matures spiritually, they feel at one with everything around them; they learn to trust and experience the moment.

"I am thankful for

My enthusiasm for all of the wonderful possibilities that exist in the world
My imagination and insights
My resourcefulness and optimism
My emphasis on striving to be all I can be

In the storms of life, I can find shelter by

Quieting down, removing the busy distractions from my life
Allowing myself to rest to nurture my soul
Focusing on what is truly of value to me

To honor myself and my pathway to God, I can

> Give free reign to my imagination as I find creative options for soulwork
> Develop my own spiritual philosophy from the many avenues I explore
> Carve out small amounts of time alone for reflection or prayer to listen for the inner voice that comes from God"
> *Soul Types*, page 137

ENFP Prayer: God, help me to keep my mind on one th—look, a bird!—ing at a time.

INFP   Introverted Feeling/Extroverted Intuition

NAUTILUS

The theme of the Nautilus is Harmonizer/Dreamer/Healer/Romantic. They thrive on being involved in a cause or project that they idealize. They are guided by a strong sense of values. Their goal is a life-long quest to find meaning and harmony. They do not like structure, rules, details, or logic. Their driving force is their deep-felt caring and idealism toward relationships. Their idealism can also be focused toward projects, ideas, or a concern for the human potential. Their motto is, "Who am I?" This becomes a question that they will seek the answer to throughout their lives.

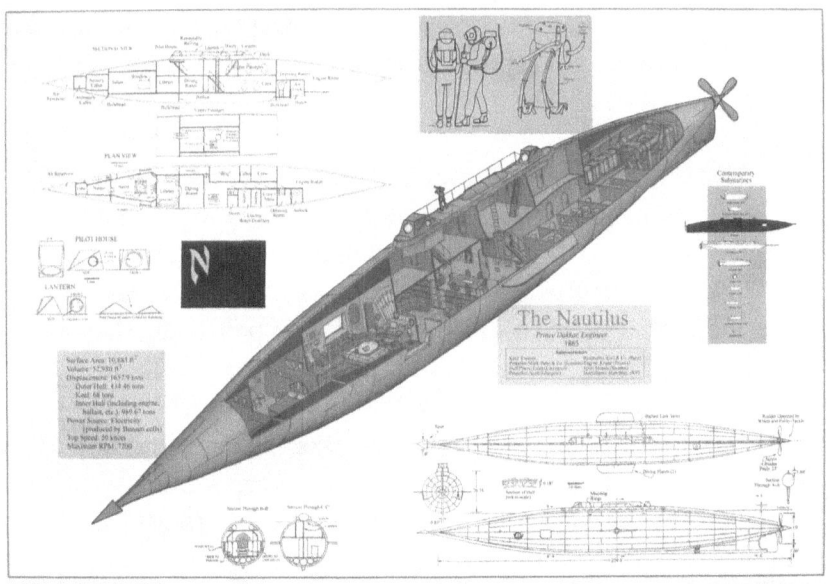

Drawing of Nautilis courtesy of Ron Miller, illustrator

I chose the *Nautilus* to represent the Dreamer/Healer/Romantic because the *Nautilus* is fantasy and hides itself in the depths of the ocean. There is one quote that cemented my choice; it is a quote from Captain Nemo explaining why he lives isolated beneath the sea:

"Ah, monsieur, to live in the bosom of the sea! Only there can independence be found! There I recognize no master! There I am free!" *(pages 77-78)*

And that is a good description of how the Dreamer/Healer/Romantic feels—free only when deep inside themselves.

Captain Nemo also had strong values, even though they were a bit unorthodox. He also contained a great and hidden passion inside himself. Captain Nemo disregarded the rules of society and escaped in the *Nautilus*—a boat which was considered a fantasy idea at that time.

Another quote from *Twenty Thousand Leagues Under the Sea* that represents the Nautilus personality is what Captain Nemo answers when asked why he is keeping the people on board from the other ship that he had destroyed:

"No, monsieur, it is clemency. You are my prisoners of war. I am keeping you here, although one simple order would suffice to have you thrown into the bottomless ocean! You attacked me! You have stumbled on a secret that no man on earth shall ever penetrate, the secret of my whole existence. And you imagine that I am going to send you back to that world which must never hear of me again! That is out of the question! In keeping you, I am not guarding you, I am protecting myself!" *(page 73)*

The Nautilus personality guards and protects its inner self from others at all costs.

Captain Nemo and the *Nautilus* were ahead of their time, as was Jules Verne, the author. Imagination, hidden depths, fanciful, the unknown: Captain Nemo and the Nautilus both appear calm, reserved, but inside both of them are many treasures and hidden passions that few ever get to know or experience. We also discover that Captain Nemo is a man with extremely romanticized feelings hidden in the very depths of his being. He has passion and intensity—not seen by others, but always there beneath the surface.

You can spot a Nautilus by noticing that they are creative, imaginative, and passionate but manage to keep their passion fairly well hidden. You only see this deep feeling and excitement when they are discussing one of their projects or causes about which they feel strongly. They are very cautious and private individuals and do not participate in discussions, yet when everyone else has finished talking about a subject or problem, they come out with a very creative solution that had occurred to no one else. They see the "big picture" and put all the pieces together while others discuss the details. They are mainly focused toward possibilities. They also can be "original" dressers, with their own style of clothes.

Feelings play a very large part in the life of a Nautilus; in fact, they pretty much are fueled by intense feeling. But like a true Nautilus, these feelings are beneath the surface, coming up for exposure only when it will benefit one of their causes in their service to humanity or family.

The Nautilus keeps itself mainly hidden, with all of its creativity and imagination hidden inside. Their lives are inner journeys filled with spirituality, strong values, deep caring, fantasies, daydreams, ideals, and intense feelings. They can appear shy or easily confused, but beneath the surface beats the heart of a different drummer. They are curious and quick to see possibilities. Indeed, they may see the possibilities more clearly than they see the facts that are directly in front of them. They have a great interest in life's mysteries, and they love to explore the unknown.

Their speech is unique and filled with metaphors. The factual and logic-based personalities often discredit the Nautilus as being "fanciful" or "out there", but in doing so, they miss the great insights and possibilities that exist in whatever is being discussed. They are able to combine and mix topics with an intuitiveness that shows possibilities that others miss. Their speech and thoughts are filled with connections between opposites and interpretations, discussing things that can only be seen within the depths of their minds. When a Nautilus says, "This 'whatever the topic is' reminds me of 'something completely opposite or unrelated,'" pay attention—because the connection is usually relevant and important.

Many times, a Nautilus personality will have difficulty putting into words exactly what they want to say. This may be because they have been misinterpreted and misunderstood so much in their lives. This leads them to either over-explaining everything, going back and saying the same thing in many different ways, or, not speaking at all. Writing becomes an outlet for them because writing allows them to put onto paper what they could not say in speech.

Examples of Nautilus personalities are Isabel Briggs Myers (the creator of the Myers-Briggs Profile Indicator), James Taylor, Carl Rogers, Neil Diamond, Princess Diana, and Jim Croce. In fiction, they are represented by Deanna Troi in *Star Trek* and Calvin in *Calvin and Hobbes*, and also by the writer who wrote Calvin and Hobbes, Bill Watterson.

Isabel Briggs Myers

An Introvert, she worked alone, taking each of Jung's propositions seriously and finding ways from her own experience to use and extend them. Her Extraverted Intuition was ever alert to new meanings, new patterns, and new insights.

In conversation, she was always appreciative and interested, never critical. It was not wise to be lulled into complacency by her warm approbation, however. If you used a negative adjective to describe a type, she gently substituted another adjective with the same intent, but with a neutral tone. "You mentioned pig-headed. Did you mean firm?" If you assumed she was talking "arm-chair philosophy" on a point, you found there were months of work and analysis behind her statements. She cared deeply about her work and fought for it against all criticisms. If data showed her wrong, she was all attention. She now had a new problem to solve to improve the Indicator. She never ceased her search for perfection.

"I dream that long after I'm gone, my work will go on helping people" (Isabel Myers, 1979).

From small beginnings four decades earlier, through long, solitary years of painstaking research and development, Isabel Myers saw, at the end of her life, acceptance and appreciation of her work. Much more important to her was the certainty that what she had created would indeed go on to enrich millions of lives in the years to come.

CAPT (Center for Applications of Psychological type, info@capt.org). C. J. Jung is the founder of the idea of Psychological types: Isabel Briggs Myers created the Myers-Briggs Type Indicator᾿ instrument based on the theories of Carl Gustav Jung.

C.J. Jung:
"The psyche is part of the inmost mystery of life, and it has its own structure and form like every other organism."

"If one reflects upon what consciousness really is, one is deeply impressed by the extremely wonderful fact that an event which occurs within the cosmos produces simultaneously an inner image, thus it also occurs within, so to speak: in other words, it becomes conscious."

"I cannot prove to you that God exists, but my work has proved empirically that and that this pattern in the individual has at its disposal the greatest transforming energies of which life is capable. Find this pattern in your own individual self and life is transformed."

"Your vision will become clear only when you look into your heart... Who looks outside, dreams. Who looks inside, awakens."

"This is old age, and a limitation. Yet there is so much that fills me: plants, animals, clouds, day and night, and the eternal in man. The more uncertain I have felt about myself, the more there has grown up in me a feeling of kinship with all things. In fact, it seems to me as if that alienation which so long separated me from the world has become transferred into my own inner world, and has revealed to me an unexpected unfamiliarity with myself. "

"What is essential in a work of art is that it should rise far above the realm of personal life and speak to the spirit and heart of the poet as man to the spirit and heart of mankind."

"Show me a sane man and I will cure him for you."

"Knowing your own darkness is the best method for dealing with the darknesses of other people."

"I could not say I believe. I know! I have had the experience of being gripped by something that is stronger than myself, something that people call God."

"All the works of man have their origin in creative fantasy. What right have we then to depreciate imagination?"

"As far as we can discern, the sole purpose of human existence is to kindle a light in the darkness of mere being."

"Everything that irritates us about others can lead us to an understanding of ourselves."

"I cannot love anyone if I hate myself. That is the reason why we feel so extremely uncomfortable in the presence of people who are noted for their special virtuousness, for they radiate an atmosphere of the torture they inflict on themselves. That is not a virtue but a vice."

"In all chaos there is a cosmos, in all disorder a secret order."

"The debt we owe to the play of imagination is incalculable."

"The meeting of two personalities is like the contact of two chemical substances: if there is any reaction, both are transformed."

"Through pride we are ever deceiving ourselves. But deep down below the surface of the average conscience, a still, small voice says to us, something is out of tune."

"Without this playing with fantasy, no creative work has ever yet come to birth. The debt we owe to the play of the imagination is incalculable."

James Taylor:
"Sweet dreams and flying machines in pieces on the ground."

"The secret to life is enjoying the passage of time."

"Though the body sleeps, the heart will never rest."

"Shower the people you love with love, show them the way that you feel. Things are going to work out fine, if you only will."

"Do me wrong, do me right, tell me lies, but hold me tight."

"All invisible from where we stand / the connections come to pass, / and though too strong to comprehend / they affect us not the less."

"Turn away from your animal kind, / try to leave your body just to live in your mind."

"Within my heart is carved a sculpture of your love."

Carl Rogers
"In my early professional years, I was asking the question: How can I treat, or cure, or change this person? Now I would phrase the question in this way: How can I provide a relationship which this person may use for his own personal growth?"

"The facts are always friendly; every bit of evidence one can acquire, in any area, leads one that much closer to what is true."

"The good life is a process, not a state of being. It is a direction, not a destination."

"The only person who is educated is the one who has learned how to learn and change."

"The very essence of the creative is its novelty, and hence we have no standard by which to judge it."

"The relationship which I have found helpful is characterized by a sort of transparency on my part, in which my real feelings are evident; by an acceptance of this other person as a separate person with value in his own right; and by a deep empathic understanding which enables me to see his private world through his eyes."

"The curious paradox is that when I accept myself just as I am, then I can change."

"If we value independence, if we are disturbed by the growing conformity of knowledge, of values, of attitudes, which our present system induces, then we may wish to set up conditions of learning which make for uniqueness, for self-direction, and for self-initiated learning."

"What I am is good enough if I would only be it openly."

Neil Diamond:
"I came back to performing with a different attitude about performing and myself. I wasn't expecting perfection anymore, just hoping for an occasional inspiration."

"It's very difficult for me to say 'I love you,' but to sing 'I love you' for me is easier."

"I followed all life's pleasures wherever they would lead / But someone I can treasure is all I really need."

"Nothing is sadder than love left unheard."

"When love is unkind, it is not love anymore."

"I am, I cried. I am, I said. And I am lost."

"Hands, touching hands, reaching out, touching me, touching you."

"You are the sun, I am the moon / You are the words, I am the tune. / Play me."

"I am, I said to no one there / And no one heard at all, not even a chair."

"Be as a page that aches for a word, which speaks on a theme that is timeless."
Lyrics source listed in Bibliography

Princess Diana
"Anywhere I see suffering, that is where I want to be, doing what I can."

"Every one of us needs to show how much we care for each other and, in the process, care for ourselves."

"Helping people in need is a good and essential part of my life, a kind of destiny."

"I am all about caring. I have always been like that."

"I am not a political figure, nor do I want to be one; but I come with my heart."

"I don't go by the rule book... I lead from the heart, not the head."

"I don't want expensive gifts; I don't want to be bought. I have everything I want. I just want someone to be there for me, to make me feel safe and secure."

"I like to be a free spirit. Some don't like that, but that's the way I am."

"I think the biggest disease the world suffers from in this day and age is the disease of people feeling unloved. I know that I can give love for a minute, for half an hour, for a day, for a month, but I can give. I am very happy to do that. I want to do that."

"I want to walk into a room, be it a hospital for the dying or a hospital for the sick children, and feel that I am needed. I want to do, not just to be."

"I wear my heart on my sleeve."

"I will fight for my children on any level so they can reach their potential as human beings and in their public duties."

"I'd like to be a queen in people's hearts, but I don't see myself being queen of this country."

"I'm aware that people I have loved and have died and are in the spirit world looking after me."

"I've got to have a place where I can find peace of mind."

"If you find someone you love in your life, then hang on to that love."

"It is a weakness that I lead from my heart, and not my head?"

"Only do what your heart tells you."

"Perhaps we're too embarrassed to change or too frightened of the consequences of showing that we actually care. But why not risk it anyway? Begin today. Carry out a random act of seemingly senseless kindness, with no expectation of reward or punishment. Safe in the knowledge that one day, someone somewhere might do the same for you."

Jim Croce:

"If I had a box just for wishes and dreams that had never come true / the box would be empty, except for the memory of how they were answered by you."

"Lost my ideals in that tunnel of time."

"I've overcome the blow, I've learned to take it well. I only wish my words could just convince myself, but that's not the way it feels."

"A fool I am and I'll always be. / They can change their minds, but they can't change me."

"Every time I tried to tell you / the words just came out wrong, / so I'll have to say 'I love you' in a song."

"If I could save time in a bottle / the first thing I'd like to do / is to save every day 'til eternity passes away / just to spend them with you."

"Bridges are meant for burning / when the people and memories they join aren't the same."

Lyrics source listed in Bibliography

Deanna Troi

"I am the Goddess of Empathy! Cast off your inhibitions and embrace love, truth, joy!"

"Cast aside your masks and let me slip into your mind."

"Words are here—on top. What's under them, their meaning . . . is what's important."

"You can't be open to love if you don't risk pain."

"We still have to learn how to live in the real world, mother, all of us."

Bill Watterson
"My strip is about private realities, the magic of imagination, and the specialness of certain friendships. Who would believe in the innocence of a little kid and his tiger if they cashed in on their popularity to sell overpriced knickknacks that nobody needs?"

"Calvin Creator's Secret Hideout: Cartoonist Bill Watterson Returns to a Cloistered Life"
(*The Plain Dealer*, Cleveland, Ohio, December 20, 1998)
John C. Kuehner Plain Dealer Reporter

Shhh. A publicity-shy artist is living in this village, and you don't want to scare him away.

Bill Watterson, the reclusive creator of "Calvin and Hobbes," has come home, and he prefers that no one know it.

It has been almost three years since Calvin and Hobbes rode a toboggan off the comic pages to go exploring. And Watterson would like it if the two of them would just go on without him.

"He would like it all to fade away," said his father, Jim, a patent lawyer, the same profession as Calvin's dad, who was satirized often in the strip. "He doesn't get his kicks by being famous. He was just doing something he enjoyed doing."

The 40-year-old Watterson declined a formal interview.

But in a conversation at his door, where he would not allow any notes to be taken, Watterson stressed that he does not want to live, nor should he have to live, in a fish bowl or have to deal with intrusions into his life by the curious.

Calvin Quotes:

"Life's disappointments are harder to take when you don't know any swear words."

"I like maxims that don't encourage behavior modification."

"Reality continues to ruin my life."

"I'm a simple man, Hobbes."
"You?? Yesterday you wanted a nuclear powered car that could turn into a jet with laser-guided heat-seeking missiles!"
"I'm a simple man with complex tastes."

"I'm not going to do my maths homework. Look at these unsolved problems. Here's a number in mortal combat with another. One of them is going to get subtracted. But why? What will be left of him? If I answered these, it would kill the suspense. It would resolve the conflict and turn intriguing possibilities into boring old facts."
"I never really thought about the literary possibilities of math."
"I prefer to savor the mystery."

"To make a bad day worse, spend it wishing for the impossible."

"I think we dream so we don't have to be apart so long. If we're in each other's dreams, we can be together all the time."

"History is the fiction we invent to persuade ourselves that events are knowable and that life has order and direction."

"Talking with you is sort of the conversational equivalent of an out-of-body experience."

Personal Nautilus people I know are Bonny, Gerry, Carmen, and myself. Even though Nautilus personalities are a very small percentage of the population, since I am one, I have made it a quest to meet others. After all, our quest is the search for Self, so meeting others like me seemed like a good place to start—or continue. I am very much inside myself, even though most people are unaware of this. I sometimes feel as if no one really knows me because there is so much I keep inside. I did learn recently though that I can say in writing what I would never say in person. E-mails can be dangerous for Nautilus people.

Bonny is a very quiet and shy type of person—until you are able to visit down inside her Nautilus. There, she is creative, funny, imaginative, caring, and full of fantastic ideas—yes, romantic fantasies too. We are able to speak in Nautilus terms with each other, terms that no one else seems to understand. Sometimes we both yearn for more "normal" personalities. Maybe "normal" isn't the correct word; maybe it is "acceptable" personalities that we yearn for.

Gerry is my preacher and friend—aren't preachers *supposed* to be friends? Well, he is both, exuding all the warmth and caring and metaphysical possibilities that a true Nautilus should have. Gerry's "mentor" is Merlin. In one service, he made the statement that his granddaughter asked his wife, "Is Grandpa Gerry really a grown-up?" My answer to that is *"No*, and I hope he never is!"

Carmen teaches the "Course of Miracles" class that I attend, and she is also my friend. I don't have many friends, but the ones I do have are very close and dear to me. It is interesting that so many of them are Nautilus personalities. Carmen is trying very hard to let her inner self out into the world, and I believe she is doing it one step at a time.

Every time she believes she is being herself, she discovers a whole new dimension of herself that she has to get acquainted with in order to release it from its inner realm. She is very passionate about the Course of Miracles and in helping others to find their own understanding of it. She is also an artist who paints beautiful paintings of angels.

In their careers, you will find Nautilis people as poets, musicians, writers, teachers, booksellers, librarians, counselors, mediators, professors, photographers, missionaries, journalists, and researchers. When you work with a Nautilus, you will probably not be immediately aware of it, but when you know what to look for, you will begin to see them. They will be the co-worker who comes up with ideas that seem completely out of context, until you really stop and look at it. A Nautilus prefers to work alone and will become completely engrossed in a project, so much so that they will tune everyone and everything else out.

A Nautilus will have many different types of people among its fleet of friends. They do not allow many people to become really close and see what is beneath the surface, but with these select few, they become very close and form lasting relationships. They are intensely loyal and caring, and are known for their true caring and ability to connect and feel empathy toward other people. They are called "Healers" because of their ability to connect and understand where you are coming from.

If you are in a relationship with a Nautilus, you will be surprised at the depth of their caring and loyalty toward you. They are idealists, and you are no exception. They have a very romanticized ideal that they look for in a partner; they are on a constant quest to find a soulmate, one who will understand them and with whom they can share their inner world. Once they find you, they will place you on a pedestal— and will do everything within their power to keep their image of you consistent with that pedestal. They will retain that pride and romanticized image they have of you over time. They are extremely flexible and adaptable, and will find a way to fit into whatever lifestyle you prefer. But they do need their "alone" time. They will be happy to give you the personal space you need, because it is something they identify with. They will have an enormous sensitivity to your moods and feelings, and they will respond with unconditional love, even protection if needed. Because, as quiet as these people are, when a value or a loved one is threatened, they become extremely outspoken and defensive of them.

A Nautilus truly abhors conflict and anger and will submerge its feelings in order to keep the peace. Criticism is another area that will create deep feelings within the Nautilus. They see any criticism as a personal attack on who they are, and will react in very emotional and even irrational ways to the perceived personal attack against themselves.

What a Nautilus needs from others:

- Respect their need for creativity and "thinking outside the box."

- Be open to looking at things in a new way.

- Overlook their messiness and unfinished projects.

- Engage in "dream planning" activities with them about the future.

- Respect their feelings.

- Allow them time and space to figure out what they want to say.

- Respect their need to be reminded that you love them.

You will know when a Nautilus is feeling overwhelmed when they begin isolating themselves, making very critical and negative remarks about themselves, becoming closed off to new ideas or information, or throwing out idea after idea that doesn't seem to make a lot of sense (what I call "going into explanation mode").

You can help them by encouraging them to talk through their emotional state, to look outside of themselves for new information (research the topic of concern), and to look at the situation in a logical manner.

If you are a Nautilus and you notice yourself becoming overwhelmed you can help yourself by:

- Talking the situation over with a trusted friend.

- Discuss, or write down, the pros and cons of the alternative courses of action.

- Develop a logical plan.

- Exercise—do something to get out of your mind. Attend yoga, do Tai-Chi-Qui-Gong, dance, work out, or even take a walk.

- Adopt more realistic expectations.

- Engage in activities that require logic—games, mysteries, etc.

- Ask yourself, "What does my heart say? What is true for me?"

- Meditate.

- Make your needs known to others—reach out to friends.

- Journal.

Exercises that may be helpful:

Journaling is an exercise that can be very useful because you may find that you can write more clearly what you are unable to say out loud. So write about your situation or concern, describing the good points and bad, and your feelings on the subject. Be sure to include what you would like to see happen so that you can check where your thoughts are against what is "real," or possible.

Notice when you withdraw from people or events, or when you are just reluctant to say what you are thinking. What is it that you are protecting yourself from? What is the worst that could happen if you allow yourself to be with people, or to say what you are thinking? Can you think of anything good that might come from it?

In times of crisis, a Nautilus needs to talk to and be with other people. They need to focus their thoughts outside of their own minds and onto activities that require analysis and strategy, like cards or chess. If they are not able to be with other people at first, even reading a book that requires thinking can be helpful.

The Nautilus regards spirituality as an ongoing journey. They are drawn to beliefs of a mystical nature, because to them unseen and synchronistic experiences already make up the center of everyday life. Other people are often drawn to the Nautilus to discuss their secrets and confidences because Nautilus people are good listeners, have an obvious concern for nurturing others, and are open to the unexplainable. Spirituality can provide them with connections to others of a similar spiritual nature. But they are alert for judgmentalism, intolerance, or restrictions on the part of any organized religious communities in which they may find themselves. They like to meditate, study different paths of spirituality, live consistently with their values, and share with others in times of need. In fact, as they mature in their spirituality they will begin sharing themselves more freely with others from the very depths of their hearts. They will learn to feel and experience that connection and to know, deep within themselves, that we are all one.

"I am thankful for

My idealism and hope for the world

My intense ideas which provide me energy to live life deeply and abundantly
My ever-present awareness of the beauty and synchronicity of life's experiences
The way I value the importance of the spiritual journey and the things that give meaning to life

In the storms of life, I can find shelter by

Asking, "What is most important to me?"—and then making a change, sometimes even a radical change
Using a trusted person to help me see things objectively
Dialoguing with myself through journaling, art, or meditating while walking in nature

To honor myself and my pathway to God, I can

Create solitude to tap into my awareness of the spiritual part of my life
Live with personal authenticity and integrity
Add logic and objectivity to my life in order to more clearly understand my heartfelt soulwork" *Soul Types*, page 300

INFP Prayer: God, help me finish everything I sta

Section 6
NTs—Rationals

Rationals/Conceptualizers focus on the big picture and the future like Idealists, but are also logical and objective decision makers; this combination makes them more independent than the other styles. These are the superachievers, and they have a strong drive for accomplishment. They usually accomplish whatever it is they set their minds to doing. In order to feel good about themselves, they need to come across as resourceful, self-sufficient, and determined. They are usually skeptical and need lots of backed-up proof before they believe in something. They can be outwardly calm, but may be filled with great passion. They can be enthusiastic, persuasive, and convincing visionaries. They can imagine alternatives that others miss—both positive and negative. They can see the possibilities inherent in a plan—or the flaws, in which case they can nitpick it to death.

They have been defined as pragmatic, no-nonsense type of people. They are always looking for the best way to get what they want for the least amount of effort. They are not lazy; they just don't want to waste their time. They are extremely skeptical towards everything and place a layer of doubt over every undertaking. And this applies not only to their own ventures, but to whatever their friends or family members are involved in too.

In one book, I read that Rationals do not view time as the other personality styles do. Experiencers see time as Now, Traditionalists/ Guardians see time in relation to the past, and Idealists see tomorrow. To Rationalists, time is an event, a segment connected to an event. They lose track of the clock and become completely engulfed in the event that they are involved in.

The Rationals are:

Aircraft Carrier

Sailboat

Houseboat

Submersible

ENTJ Extraverted Thinking with Intuiting

AIRCRAFT CARRIER

Their theme is Leader/Strategist/Field Marshall. They thrive on marshalling forces. Their goal is to command and establish plans. Their battle cry can often be heard as "Let's everybody work together to do it my way." Their driving force is their need to analyze and bring the people, events, and things around them into a logical order. They can have an almost military approach to their families and their careers.

I have chosen a military boat, the aircraft carrier, to represent their personality. They are powerful, domineering, decisive, and confrontational. They believe in putting pressure on people in order to reach goals. Their Intuiting approach steers their thinking to the future and what needs to be done.

You will recognize an Aircraft Carrier by its high-energy, take-charge attitude. They are fearless, dominant organized, and driven. In any group, they will become the leader and strategist, pulling the rest of the group together by confidently establishing goals with their systematic and analytical objectives. They are good at inspiring others with their confidence and compelling energy. These are the people who provide structure, have high expectations, see the big picture, and believe in seeing that fairness prevails.

Examples of Aircraft Carriers listed in the literature are Newt Gingrich, Napoleon, Margaret Thatcher, and Steve Martin. I also believe that General George S. Patton exemplifies the characteristics of an Aircraft Carrier. Below are several quotes that demonstrate these ideas.

General George Patton:
"By perseverance, study, and eternal desire, any man can become great."

"Do everything you ask of those you command."

"Do more than is required of you."

"If everybody is thinking alike, then somebody isn't thinking."

"If I do my full duty, the rest will take care of itself."

"There is only one type of discipline, perfect discipline."

"A man must know his destiny... if he does not recognize it, then he is lost. By this I mean, once, twice, or at the very most, three times, fate will reach out and tap a man on the shoulder... if he has the imagination, he will turn around and fate will point out to him what fork in the road he should take. If he has the guts, he will take it."

Newt Gingrich:
"Perseverance is the hard work you do after you get tired of doing the hard work you already did."

"Politics and war are remarkably similar situations."

"You have to give the press confrontations. When you give them confrontations, you get attention; when you get attention, you can educate."

Napoleon:
"I am sometimes a fox and sometimes a lion. The whole secret of government lies in knowing when to be the one or the other."

"I can no longer obey; I have tasted command, and I cannot give it up."

"I have only one counsel for you—be master."

"I made all my generals out of mud."

"If I always appear prepared, it is because before entering an undertaking, I have meditated long and have foreseen what might occur. It is not genius which reveals to me suddenly and secretly what I should do in circumstances unexpected by others; it is thought and preparation."

"If you start to take Vienna—take Vienna."

"If you wish to be a success in the world, promise everything, deliver nothing."

"If you want a thing done well, do it yourself."

"Impossible is a word to be found only in the dictionary of fools."

"Nothing is more difficult, and therefore more precious, than to be able to decide."

"Power is my mistress. I have worked too hard at her conquest to allow anyone to take her away from me."

"The act of policing is, in order to punish less often, to punish more severely."

Margaret Thatcher:
"Being powerful is like being a lady. If you have to tell people you are, you aren't."

"Disciplining yourself to do what you know is right and important, although difficult, is the highroad to pride, self-esteem, and personal satisfaction."

"I am extraordinarily patient, provided I get my own way in the end."

"I don't mind how much my Ministers talk, so long as they do what I say."

"I shan't be pulling the levers there, but I shall be a very good back-seat driver."

"I usually make up my mind about a man in ten seconds, and I very rarely change it."

"If you lead a country like Britain, a strong country, a country which has taken a lead in world affairs in good times and in bad, a country that is always reliable, then you have to have a touch of iron about you."

"If you set out to be liked, you would be prepared to compromise on anything at any time, and you would achieve nothing."

"If you want something said, ask a man; if you want something done, ask a woman."

"Pennies do not come from heaven. They have to be earned here on earth."

"Standing in the middle of the road is very dangerous; you get knocked down by the traffic from both sides."

"Success is having a flair for the thing that you are doing; knowing that is not enough, that you have got to have hard work and a sense of purpose."

"To wear your heart on your sleeve isn't a very good plan; you should wear it inside, where it functions best."

Steve Martin:
"An apology? Bah! Disgusting! Cowardly! Beneath the dignity of any gentleman, however wrong he might be."

"I believe entertainment can aspire to be art, and can become art, but if you set out to make art, you're an idiot."

Also, many CEOs of big corporations are comprised of this type of boat. It takes their drive, strategy, and outspoken assertiveness to reach those positions.

I have known only one Aircraft Carrier in my life; he was one of my ex-husbands. I would like to use someone else as an example, but he is the only one I have known personally. Stan is definitely the take-charge type. He is very friendly and outgoing, even charismatic, and he grasps situations and ideas quickly. He always has several projects going at once. In fact, he is the one who made the statement that "Some people wait for their ship to come in, but they haven't sent any out there. Me, I have a whole fleet out there!" Stan is very creative and innovative; he is very bright and knowledgeable. He does have a tendency to believe that his way of doing things is the only way to do them. And, yes, he can be condescending and arrogant to others if they are seen as beneath him, or have the audacity to disagree with his way of seeing things. As far as vacations, well, he doesn't really like them. The only vacation he likes is one that is connected with sending another boat out to join the rest of his fleet. Being an INFP, I am not assertive or detail-oriented enough to communicate in a style that he can understand.

In careers, you will often see Aircraft Carriers as leaders and executive officers in their companies. If they aren't the leaders yet, you can be sure they will be headed in that direction. They have a plan, they know the right way to get things done, and they are determined to show everyone how to get the job done. If you work for an Aircraft Carrier, keep in mind that they are extremely impatient with inefficiency and incompetence. You will be permitted to make a mistake—but please, never make the same mistake twice. You will be recognized for your hard work, especially in regards in sticking with the well-structured plans put in place by the Aircraft Carrier.

As friends, Aircraft Carriers will provide highly stimulating and dynamic interactions. They will be intensely interested in your ideas and perspectives; they love learning and enlarging their perspectives. They will often be found in lively and challenging conversations, debating issues with enthusiasm. They will often approach people in an interrogative mode, trying to learn their reasoning and strategy behind their stance and beliefs. So if you are friends with an Aircraft Carrier, know your facts and your logic behind what you say, because you will be put on the spot and need to explain your reasoning. These conversations are highly stimulating and appreciated by the Aircraft Carrier; they feel they have learned another approach to their constant drive to improve strategic thinking and direction.

If you have found yourself in a relationship with an Aircraft Carrier, you will need to be able to keep up by providing an atmosphere of continual learning and growth. You will be expected to follow their lead and live by their rules. In exchange, you will have found a very committed partner. They won't always notice your feelings or express gratitude as often as you would like, but you will live a very comfortable and exciting lifestyle. Even though you will be expected to follow the rules established by the Aircraft Carrier, remember that they like innovative and challenging ideas, so you will need to keep your ideas creative and interesting in the approach you make to follow those rules.

What an Aircraft Carrier needs from you:

- Keep your life together orderly.

- Listen to the advice they give on how things should be done.

- Stay interesting and innovative to keep them on their toes.

- Be unemotional, factual, and detailed when problems arise.

- Get to the point when you have a complaint.

If you are in a relationship with an Aircraft Carrier and you notice that they are becoming either overly rigid or uncharacteristically emotional or illogical—some have even been known to believe others are out to "get them"—it is a sign that they are becoming overwhelmed. You can help them best by encouraging them to slow down, to get in touch with what is going on inside, and maybe to spend some time in introspection to help them see things in a different way.

If you are an Aircraft Carrier and are having problems because of your style, causing you to feel powerless, paranoid, or frustrated, here are some suggestions that may help you:

- Sit quietly with a problem before making a decision. Allow yourself to reflect on the issue at hand.

- Check to see how others have interpreted your actions and/or words.

- Allow other people their spaces and ways of doing things too.

- Don't try to be who you are not. Express yourself in ways that are real to you.

- Don't blame other people for the problem you have.

- If you cannot see or understand how you are affecting others, get a friend whom you trust to provide their viewpoint. There are usually not a lot of people you can be open with, but developing that type of friend could be one of the things that could be helpful.

- Examine your expectations of rejection.

Exercises that may be helpful:

Look at the situations where you are unable to back down with others. Were there times in your past where you faced similar incidents? How did you feel? What did it take for you to feel that you had "won" the situation?

Look at a situation where you pressured someone to do something differently than they wanted to do. Can you think of another way you could have approached the situation differently than you did? What if that person had done it "your way" without your having had to pressure them? Also, look at times when someone has tried to pressure you. How did you feel? React?

In times of crisis, Aircraft Carriers need to look inside themselves at what is going on with themselves physically. They get so caught up in what they are doing that they don't eat, sleep, exercise, or rest properly; their health can suffer. Helping an Aircraft Carrier to stop looking around outside of themselves at ideas and strategies and to start looking inside to feel, sense, and think is not an easy task. But it's one that the Aircraft Carrier will eventually have to do in order to become that complete person that they want to be.

The Aircraft Carrier will approach spirituality like they do everything else, with lots of energy, lots of questioning, and looking for ways that can bring people together to accomplish goals—a plan of action! In their spiritual life, they will be drawn to paths that will allow and encourage them to use their natural skepticism and challenging attitude. They will thrive on debates about beliefs, even helping those around them become more clearly set on their own path. As an Aircraft Carrier matures into their full spirituality, they begin to see that they don't have to demand or get their way—their attitude changes from me-against-the world to understanding that they have a role to play in the world—to just be themselves.

"I am thankful for

My mind, which sees solutions and strategies where others see turmoil
My quest for truth and clarity, adding insights to each endeavor
My commitment to excellence in everything I undertake
The way I lead people toward well-defined goals

In the storms of life, I can find shelter by

Taking time out to explore alternative possibilities and solutions
Discovering what matters most to me and those I value
Considering the experiences of others and asking for their help

To honor myself and my pathway to God, I can

Satisfy my need to know—my desire to understand our universe and ultimately our creator

175

Define and accept a logical basis for what I take on faith—be able to intellectualize this intangible part of our being
Find ways to bring my soulwork to bear on my relationships with others and with God" *Soul Types*, page 203

ENTJ Prayer: God, today I have a plan; let's see that it gets done—and done right.

INTJ   Introverted Intuiting with Thinking

SAILBOATS

A Sailboat's theme is Conceptualizer/Director/Mastermind. They thrive on visualizing the long-term plan. Their goal is to gain insight, awareness, and understanding of the things they choose to study. They are driven by inner ideas and possibilities; they tend to think systematically. Their theme is innovation and independence; they tend to steer through life by their own internal compass. Their motto is, "I'm doing it my way."

Where to put the Sailboat was an interesting decision—everybody wants to be a sailboat. But I decided on the Conceptualizer/Mastermind because they are both driven by innovation, independence, and possibilities. They have a driving need to *understand;* they want to both know and be able to show competence in anything that interests them. They do it "their way."

Sailboats are free and natural. It's the process that is important to them. These are the people who like to build their own businesses. The enjoyment for them is in the planning, the bringing it all together, and the using their own ability to make *something* from *nothing*. It is their skill, their strength, and their determination that lead them through life. These are the free spirits in life who travel by their own inner drummer. They have original minds and a strong inner drive for their own ideas and purposes. They are independent and have high standards of competence and performance. These people add a touch of naturalness and genuineness to your life. When you are involved with a Sailboat, you will learn a lot about yourself and learn to enjoy the simple, more natural life. A Sailboat will *never* own a digital watch; only "natural" watches will do.

There are many different styles of sailboats, from the small dinghy to the impressively large tall ships. All of them incorporate naturalness and a love of freedom as a basis of operation. They can be rather single-minded, though.

For those of you who watched *Home Improvement,* Tim Taylor's neighbor, Wilson, would illustrate a Sailboat personality. Wilson is a person who enjoys all that life has to offer. He repeatedly helps Tim (and sometimes Jill) by bringing calmness into their lives. Wilson finds pleasure in doing everything naturally. The journey is Wilson's enjoyment, not just the goal. As an example, he doesn't just *like* honey, but the entire process of the bees *making* honey; Wilson would have his own beehive.

Katherine Hepburn would also fit in this category. She was very much her own person, and loved doing things naturally and in her own way.

Can't you just see Katherine Hepburn with her face turned toward the wind, sailing through the seas of her life?

Other examples of Sailboat personalities listed in the literature are Phil Donahue, Chevy Chase, and the fictional character Clarice Starling.

Katherine Hepburn:
From *"Tribute to Katherine Hepburn"* by Sharon Levine Waldman:
Another big part of her significance is the impact she had as a role model for women. Her unique persona captured the public's imagination, and the parts she played reflected a new kind of woman: confident, independent, and able to hold her own with a strong male partner."
Kate was lean and athletic and liked to do her own stunts.
She refused projects she didn't like, buying out her contract to avoid doing lesser projects.
Hepburn flouted fashion's rules, wearing slacks and sneakers when most women wore girdles, petticoats, stockings, garter belts, and high heels. "Stockings are an invention of the Devil," she declared, and refused to wear them. She wanted to be comfortable. Once, when RKO brass took away her slacks (to force her to wear a skirt), she walked around the lot in her underwear until they returned them. Kate's pants became a symbol of independence for women, liberating them to be more active and have more choices.
Hepburn's personal style, honesty, strength of spirit, and ability to live on her own have already influenced three generations of women to be more educated, more independent, and more active.
Kate and Spencer never married, not, as legend has it, because he couldn't get a divorce (he was Catholic; his wife Louise wasn't), but because it suited both of

them. Kate later mused, "Perhaps men and women should live next door and just visit now and then."

Quotes:
"I never realized until lately that women were supposed to be the inferior sex."
"Life is to be lived. If you have to support yourself, you had bloody well better find some way that is going to be interesting. And you don't do that by sitting around wondering about yourself."
"If you always do what interests you, at least one person is pleased."
"If you obey all the rules, you miss all the fun."
"Enemies are so stimulating."

Phil Donahue:
"With this terrible fear of `the L-word,' who the hell would put me on the payroll and have to handle all that flak about liberal bias in the media?" he said in a recent interview. "I honestly didn't think that barrier could be surmounted." MSNBC surmounted it, announcing that Donahue, a loud-and-proud leftie, had been hired as host.

Phil Donahue Quotes:
"I have been in the witness protection program for the last three weeks. I campaigned for Ralph Nader. I'm now living as a woman in Mississippi."

"Some people are uncomfortable with the idea that humans belong to the same class of animals as cats and cows and raccoons. They're like the people who become successful and then don't want to be reminded of the old neighborhood."

Chevy Chase:
"Growing up, Chase proved as rambunctious as he was intelligent. He was valedictorian of his high school class, but previously had been expelled from New York's elite Dalton School. He was also expelled from Haverford College for a stunt involving a cow. Eventually, he would graduate from Bard College" (AMCTV.com).

From Laker Jim's Fletch Won
Interviews with Tim Mateson

"Hey! You won't believe this, but Chevy has *finally* answered all of your questions! Unfortunately, we printed them out [and] gave them directly to Chevy, who 'lost' them in a pile, a huge pile of papers next to our bed. I've been spring cleaning and found it a couple of weeks ago. He felt so bad! He finally had some time yesterday to sit down and write out answers. He's not real good on the computer, so he still writes things out longhand. So, please respond and we'll go from there!" (Jayni Chase).

"Sorry this took so long! My e-mail is defunct. Stuff also got lost in the shuffle" (Chevy).

"Ask not what your country can do for you. Ask what you can do for...uhh...me."

"What made this [*Fletch*] my favorite picture was that I winged just about *everything* in it—particularly dialogue. But most of the time, when I wanted to do something funny, or made it up while the camera was rolling ('steak sandwich and a steak sandwich' or 'using the whole fist, Doc,' etc, etc), Mike just let the camera roll, leaving us with such anomalies as 'John Cocktoatohh...' Fletch is me."

Clarice Starling *(Hannibal Lectre & Silence of the Lambs)*:
Clarice Starling is very introspective and does things in her own way. She is very quiet and reserved, and

cool and formal in her interactions with others. She becomes excited when talking about the serial killer because it is something that is of extreme interest to her—it is her area of expertise. Her world is one of introspection and deep thoughts.

She dresses conservatively, but in a manner that fits her needs; she doesn't particularly care what others think of how she dresses. She loves a challenge; she is very independent. She is natural and follows her own drummer.

I have a friend who is a Sailboat personality, Roger. I've known Roger since I was sixteen years old, and he has *always* done his own thing—followed his own drummer. He can be both quiet and talkative. He becomes more animated and outspoken when the topic turns to a subject which he feels strongly about. He has his very strong personal opinions about many topics and is quick to let you know it. He loves lighthouses and abandoned military bases. He has many friends, and his friends are very important to him, but he usually prefers to be around them one or two at a time. Roger does own a sailboat and enjoys spending time alone it. He also likes taking one or two friends with him. He doesn't much care about doing what other people think he should do; he pretty much follows his own intuition—his own inner guidance system. And he has never worn a digital watch.

Sailboats take pride in a job well done. The trip itself is their enjoyment—not just reaching their destination. They love their work, the actual *doing* of it—and doing it well. They take pleasure in using their own natural abilities. When you work along side a Sailboat, you will find yourself slowing down and taking pleasure in the accomplishment of a job well done.

As friends, they are energetic and enjoy life. During troubled times, they can help you find your own inner calmness by helping you get back in touch with your natural instincts. They can be very spiritual individuals, although religion, as such, may put them off. They don't want to follow someone else's rules of how they should live or be in contact with God. They understand that by being in touch with their own inner guidance they have found their own way to God within themselves.

As a romantic interest, a Sailboat can be an exciting and valuable partner. They will put the effort and enjoyment into a relationship that they put into everything else that they do. They will enjoy the relationship itself. They are able to relate on a level that other styles cannot, because they are more in tune with their own internal self, their own naturalness. They expect you to be the same. No games are allowed here, only honesty.

What a Sailboat needs from you:

- Privacy and alone time.

- Appreciation of their creative and novel approaches.

- Honesty (this is important).

- To be allowed to follow "their own drummer."

If you are in a relationship with a Sailboat, you can tell they are becoming overwhelmed when they start obsessing about details, becoming hostile, or avoiding things that they normally enjoy doing.

During these times, you can best help the Sailboat by:

- Listening to what is worrying them.

- Encouraging them to participate in activities with others, especially activities which involve physical exertion.

- Helping them to take time for themselves to do something that they like to do, like a hobby for example.

If you are a Sailboat and feel yourself to be under stress, here are some suggestions that you may find helpful:

- Try to understand where other people are coming from; learn to recognize their personality type.

- When angry or upset, walk away and spend time working on a concrete task (hobby, project).

- Engage in physical exercise.

- Don't dismiss ideas without thinking them through first.

- Don't blame other people, but look inside yourself for what you can do.

- Engage in activities that are of interest to you and that are natural to you.

- Take the time to meditate and pay attention to your own internal navigational system.

- Reach out to other people. Your tendency to isolate usually only gets you deeper into your own feeling of being locked in.

Exercises that can help:

Notice how you tend to restrict yourself to certain areas of expertise and interest. Are there other areas of your life that you are neglecting because of limiting yourself to these areas? What other areas could you expand if you did not limit yourself?

Keep a record, a journal, of things that cause you to isolate. The next time you are with people, see if you can catch yourself when you start to "shut down" or begin to detach from them. What is the thought or feeling that initiates that isolation?

During a crisis, a Sailboat can relieve stress by physical activity, not work activities, but exercise—bicycling, running, swimming. During such times, though, they may find that doing neglected household tasks can be beneficial—painting that back bedroom that they never did get around to, cleaning the garage, etc. Eventually, though, they need to find an atmosphere of peaceful friends to be around, where it can become safe to learn to feel.

Many Sailboats pursue their own spirituality in solitude. They may seek to commune with God directly about what they need to do, accepting the guidance they receive inside as a gauge on how to steer their course through life. Many Sailboats prefer nature to more structured settings. But when they do choose a more structured setting, they will connect themselves in areas where planning, research, and design are necessary. Like other boats who are individualistic, the maturing spirituality of these Sailboats will lead them to a feeling of connection with life, with all that is.

"I am thankful for

My keen insights and inspirations
My love of challenges and complex problems requiring elegant approaches
My ease with systems, strategies, and structures
My determination and drive to perfect my ideas

In the storms of life, I can find shelter by

Developing a plan, then loosening control and accepting the outcome
Inviting logical feedback from a respected and trusted colleague
Giving myself ample time for play and rejuvenation

To honor myself and my pathway to God, I can

Satisfy my intellect with prayer, study, or retreat
Observe the little things right now—the momentary pleasures that can enrich my life when I take time to notice

Put my mind to work for greater purposes that serve my spiritual philosophy" *Soul Types*, page 151

INTJ Prayer: God, keep me open to other people's opinions, no matter how *incorrect* they may be.

ENTP Extroverted Intuiting with Thinking

HOUSEBOAT

A Houseboat's theme is the Visionary/Explorer/Inventor. They thrive on finding new ways to do things, and are interested in everything. Their theme is possibility; their goal is challenge and improvising. "Keep your options open" could be their battle cry. Their driving force is their excitement about involvement in anything new. They tend to have many projects going at the same time, and are always ready to pack up and move on to the next exciting challenge. One article even called them "upbeat visionaries."

I used a Houseboat to represent the Visionary—the Explorer—because they are frequently on the move, in search of new experiences. Like a real houseboat, they are willing to move on to the next port and adventure in their lives. They look for patterns in life and have a deep need to know the nature of the things in their world. They are charismatic and have the ability to persuade others to follow them into all kinds of uncharted waters. They are independent and self-contained and do not want restrictions placed upon them.

These are the people who enjoy traveling from place to place, whether it is to a new physical location or a new adventurous project. They drop anchor for short periods of time, but then after a brief rest set out on the open seas again to discover what else is out there. They like to experience many different adventures and opportunities. They are extremely flexible. Some would say that they are mercurial, whimsical or erratic. These are the people who keep their options open, looking for something new to come along. Houseboats love people and are very insightful about them. They are extremely spontaneous.

I imagine Steven Speilberg as a Houseboat personality. I don't know if he likes to pack up and move from place to place, but he does voyage from one project to another on a regular basis. He ignores traditional approaches, and he is extremely gifted in getting others excited about his ideas and projects. That's why he has made so many wonderful and varied movies. He commits himself completely to the short-term project of the movie he is making. But, when the movie is completed, he packs up his cameras and moves on to another creative idea and adventure. Variety is certainly a word that describes the undertakings of Mr. Speilberg.

> "We had snakes in Raiders of the Lost Ark and bugs in Indiana and the Temple of Doom, but supposedly man's greatest fear is public speaking. That'll be in our next picture."

> "I dream for a living."

Leonardo Da Vinci was another example of this type of personality. He was well-known for his art, but he was also involved in numerous other projects. He went from painting to sculpture to designs for helicopters; he wanted to experience everything. Of course, Mr. Da Vinci wasn't always known to complete a project before he moved on to the next one, but that can also be typical behavior of a Houseboat. He was constant searching for a "better way" and was extremely curious about how he could make things different. He certainly liked variety and could envision the future.

"Although nature commences with reason and ends in experience, it is necessary for us to do the opposite, that is, to commence with experience and from this to proceed to investigate the reason."

"Experience does not err. Only your judgments err by expecting from her what is not in her power."

"I have been impressed with the urgency of doing. Knowing is not enough; we must apply. Being willing is not enough; we must do."

"Iron rusts from disuse; water loses its purity from stagnation... even so does inaction sap the vigor of the mind."

"It had long since come to my attention that people of accomplishment rarely sat back and let things happen to them. They went out and happened to things."

"Life is pretty simple: You do some stuff. Most fails. Some works. You do more of what works. If it works big, others quickly copy it. Then you do something else. The trick is the doing something else."

"There shall be wings! If the accomplishment be not for me, 'tis for some other."

Other examples would be Walt Disney, Tom Hanks, and Wile E. Coyote. They are well-known for their vision and variety in their pursuits to reach their goals.

Quotes from or about these Houseboats which characterize their personality style:

Walt Disney:
"Disneyland will never be completed. It will continue to grow as long as there is imagination left in the world."

"If you can dream it, you can do it. Always remember that this whole thing was started with a dream and a mouse."

"It's something that will never be finished. Something that I can keep developing... and adding to."

"It's kind of fun to do the impossible."

Tom Hanks:
"I will entertain anything; it doesn't matter. You know, it's not obviously about the price, it's not about who, it's kind of about when and what."

"From now on, we live in a world where man has walked on the moon. It's not a miracle; we just decided to go."

"That's what's nice about directing a film and having it done: There's nothing more I can do about it. It's done. That's it. All I can do is let it go and hope that people are kind to it."

Wile E. Coyote:
If you've ever seen one of these cartoons, nothing else needs to be said. But if you haven't, then Mr. Coyote is unstoppable in his many ways to catch that pesky Roadrunner!

I have a couple of Houseboat friends, and I have found that whenever I talk to them, after one of their typical absences, the first thing I will ask is, "What have you been up to now?" They are continuously changing and trying new things. Doug is an example of this. In the past six years that I have known Doug, he has had at least that many different jobs. And it is not because he loses them; it is because he keeps moving on to greener pastures. Doug is extremely knowledgeable, very warm and caring, insightful and perceptive. But he is always looking toward the next idea, the next project that will be even better. When he starts a new job, you can just see the excitement, the potential, and the creativity—but then as he conquers that job, he is ready to move on to new challenges.

Houseboats are mobile, ready to pack up and experience new places and new ideas on the spur of the moment. For example, a person who likes a job that is uprooted every couple of years—they continue to have the security of the old job, but just get to move to a new location. Once they begin a new project, they become completely immersed in their work, putting in long, dedicated hours in order to reach the vision that has them motivated. Many Houseboats do not like to work for other people; they prefer the risk and adventure of having their own business or being employed on a freelance basis. They are creative, flexible, diverse, comfortable in unfamiliar situations, experience junkies, spontaneous, and improvisers.

If you work with a Houseboat, they would be the one to entrust with a project that has an identifiable end. If the project continues on and on and has no conclusion, the Houseboat will move on to bluer waters. They want to commit themselves, comfortably, to short-term projects and ideas. Then, when the task is completed, they are ready to move on to something else, searching for another new and novel experience. They have a hunger for variety and exciting challenges.

As friends, Houseboats are great. You will always have new places to see when you visit and keep in touch. They are usually fountains of varied information because they like to keep their lives full of new ideas and experiences. They are the ones who try every new fad that comes along. They want to encounter everything! They will become very involved in each new craze, fully immersing themselves in it, until the next new concept comes along. They are very versatile and fascinating individuals. You will find that they are experts in very unexpected areas because they love variety and thirst for strange and unusual experiences.

A romantic involvement with a Houseboat will provide all the comforts of home, but you will be continually on the move—either geographically or in experiences and lifestyles. Some Houseboats like to pick up and move locations on a regular basis. Others are content to stay in one place but need to change careers, or lifestyles, or hobbies. Your life will be full of variety. At times, this can be quite stressful because you will be missing the certainty of what tomorrow will bring. Just be careful that you don't get too set in your ways, or you could be one of the things that the Houseboat moves away from. If you have a Houseboat for a mate, you will inherit the responsibility of the day-to-day living fundamentals, because they will not have time or patience for those types of activities. They will be looking into the future for the next challenge.

What a Houseboat partner needs from you:

- Listen when they have new ideas and help them brainstorm possibilities.

- Encourage them to get started and become involved in new and exciting opportunities.

- Appreciate their originality and imagination.

- Respect their need to tackle new projects.

- Don't confuse them with details.

If you have a Houseboat in your life and you notice that they are beginning to avoid challenges, withdrawing from their pursuits, becoming bitter and vindictive, or starting to sleep too much or overeat, you know they are becoming overwhelmed. You can help them by reminding them to take time to be alone and search inside themselves. They need to get in touch with their feelings. Try to get them to talk to you about whatever it is that is bothering them.

If you are a Houseboat and are experiencing some of the difficulties associated with that personality style, here are some things that may be helpful:

- Give yourself time to slow down and carefully analyze the ideas you have before charging full-steam ahead into the unknown.

- Be sure to take the needs and feelings of the other people in your life into consideration before starting something new.

- Take time to look at the facts of the situation to determine who needs to do what, and when.

- Take some quiet time to restore your soul.

- Listen to other people and their interests and concerns.

- Analyze your physical responses and assess whether changes need to be made in your eating, sleeping, or lifestyle.

- Stop and look at your feelings. Are you feeling hurt? If you are, and you are stuffing it down inside, the hurt will eventually overwhelm you. Don't deny it. Look at it and face it, then decide what steps you need to take.

Exercises that may help:

Next time you begin a new project, stop and process how you feel. What are your thoughts? How do you feel about yourself? Do you feel more alive? Then allow yourself to relax, to meditate, and ask yourself the same questions.

The next time you are ready to act on an impulse, *stop*—and relax yourself by taking several deep breaths. Now pay attention and analyze your impulsive feeling. How long does the feeling last? As you pay attention to it, what are you saying to yourself?

During time of crisis, a Houseboat can feel completely "unglued" because they do not see the options that are such a big part of their personality. First, look at their health, which they tend to neglect in the process of chasing after their many plans and projects. Then teach them how to slow down and look inside themselves for peace and calm.

In the area of Spirituality, the best paths are those that allow for self-discovery, insight, and creative ways of using your observations. Since you do not like to be in a setting where there are strict rules to follow, but want to be able to seek new ideas and connections and to explore these diverse ideas with others, joining a study group that is open to novel ideas would be beneficial for you. When a Houseboat discovers their spiritual self, they quit trying to impose their plans on the world and return to a state of naturalness and ease with the world—they become like a child and see the magnificence in everything.

"I am thankful for

My energy and enthusiasm for life's challenges
My creative and innovative vision
My ability to see patterns and find solutions
The way I can synthesize divergent ideas

In the storms of life, I can find shelter by

Prioritizing my many options and concluding which best meet my life principles
Cutting out distraction and allowing space for reflection and solitude
Paying attention to and living within those rules and guidelines that I know are important to me

To honor myself and my pathway to God, I can

Seek answers, question the pat solution, and discover the spiritual truth of this world
Pay attention to *what is* and value reality for the evidence and richness it brings to my spiritual journey
Dedicate time for my spiritual practices and life"
Soul Types, page 122

ENTP Prayer: God, help me to follow established procedures today. On second thought, I'll settle for a few minutes of procedures, then doing it *my* way.

INTP Introverted Thinking with Intuiting

SUBMERSIBLE

The theme of a Submersible is Designer/Theorizer/Architect, sometimes labeled as the Thinker. They thrive on exploring new and exciting possibilities and are involved in a constant search for understanding. Their goal is to grasp the underlying principle and to bring clarity to a subject. They like to search for the perfect solution to a problem. They are usually very independent and brilliant. They value knowledge above all else. Their focus of attention is on what is possible, not on what is. Their driving force is to understand whatever has caught their attention at the moment. They love to question. Their motto is, "To go where no man has gone before."

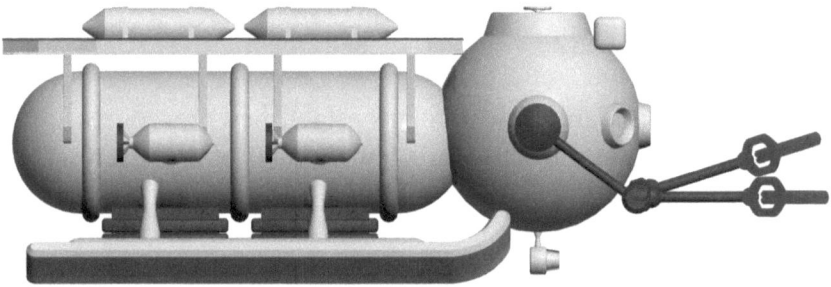

I selected a Submersible to represent a Theorizer/Thinker because submersibles are isolated, deep, scientific, and unconventional. A submersible allows its occupant(s) to go deep into the heart of the ocean, to observe things that no one has observed before. Its sole purpose is to explore and discover—and to do it in isolation and independent from others.

Socially, Submersibles are uncomfortable and tend to be guarded, allowing very few people into their world. They ignore the rules, are detached, and are often seen as eccentric. It is very hard to get to know a Submersible because they are intensely private and likely to be focused on complex thoughts and ideas. They do not like to share their ideas and thoughts with others, and these ideas and thoughts are the main focus of their lives. Submersibles spend a lot of time hidden in their own undersea world, trying to understand the world. They use this understanding to observe, describe, and ultimately explain the world to us.

A wonderful example of a Submersible would be Albert Einstein; he would be the epitome of a Submersible. He was so creative and able to see "what could be" that he represents the very essence of an unconventional and imaginative Submersible.

Below are some quotes from Albert Einstein that show his orientation as a Submersible/INTP:

> **Albert Einstein:**
> "The most beautiful thing we can experience is the mysterious. It is the source of all true art and all science. He to whom this emotion is a stranger, who can no longer pause to wonder and stand rapt in awe, is as good as dead: his eyes are closed."
> I deleted the longer quote
> "The eternal mystery of the world is its comprehensibility."
>
> "I want to know how God created this world. I am not interested in this or that phenomenon, in the spectrum of this or that element. I want to know His thoughts; the rest are details."
>
> Regarding the unified field theory, he wrote:
>
> "I cannot base this conviction on logical reasons—my only witness is the pricking of my little finger."
> "The ideals that have lighted my way, and time after time have given me new courage to face life cheerfully, have been Kindness, Beauty, and Truth. Without the sense of kinship with men of like mind, without the occupation with the objective world, the eternally unattainable in the field of art and scientific endeavors, life would have seemed empty to me. The trite objects

of human efforts—possessions, outward success, luxury—have always seemed to me contemptible.

"My passionate sense of social justice and social responsibility has always contrasted oddly with my pronounced lack of need for direct contact with other human beings and human communities. I am truly a 'lone traveler' and have never belonged to my country, my home, my friends, or even my immediate family, with my whole heart; in the face of all these ties, I have never lost a sense of distance and a need for solitude..."

"Imagination is more important than knowledge."

Other examples given in the personality style literature that fit this category would be Bob Newhart, Stephen Hawking, Richard Feynman, and Carl Sagan.

Bob Newhart:

"Laughter gives us distance. It allows us to step back from an event, deal with it and then move on."

"I don't like country music myself, but I don't mean to denigrate those who do. And for people who like country music, denigrate means 'put down.'"

Rick Moranis:

"It takes more than wearing a pen-pack to be a nerd; it also takes a certain amount of social unease. Does that also apply to Moranis? "It depends on the situation," Are there social situations where he feels really uncomfortable? "This one, right now. I feel very uncomfortable trying to come up with an answer for that question."

Rick Moranis "Comedian Under Glass" Starlog
August 1989 #145 by Jami Bernard

"I really separate the experience of doing a movie from the final product. I really put a tremendous value on the experience of doing it, which determines to a great extent how I choose my projects."

Stephen Hawking:
"Even if there is only one possible unified theory, it is just a set of rules and equations. What is it that breathes fire into the equations and makes a universe for them to describe?"

"I think computer viruses should count as life. I think it says something about human nature that the only form of life we have created so far is purely destructive. We've created life in our own image."

"My goal is simple. It is a complete understanding of the universe, why it is as it is and why it exists at all."

"Not only does God play dice, but... he sometimes throws them where they cannot be seen."

"The whole history of science has been the gradual realization that events do not happen in an arbitrary manner, but that they reflect a certain underlying order, which may or may not be divinely inspired."

"To confine our attention to terrestrial matters would be to limit the human spirit."

"We are just an advanced breed of monkeys on a minor planet of a very average star. But we can understand the Universe. That makes us something very special."

"I have hardly ever known a mathematician who was able to reason."

"When one's expectations are reduced to zero, one really appreciates everything one does have."

"It matters if you just don't give up"

"It is not clear that intelligence has any long-term survival value."

"The usual approach of science of constructing a mathematical model cannot answer the questions of why there should be a universe for the model to describe. Why does the universe go to all the bother of existing?"

"All the evidence shows that God was actually quite a gambler, and the universe is a great casino, where dice are thrown and roulette wheels spin on every occasion."

Richard Feynman:
"For a successful technology, reality must take precedence over public relations, for Nature cannot be fooled."

"I believe that a scientist looking at nonscientific problems is just as dumb as the next guy."

"I was born not knowing and have had only a little time to change that here and there."

"If I could explain it to the average person, it wouldn't have been worth the Nobel Prize."

"It doesn't matter how beautiful your theory is; it doesn't matter how smart you are. If it doesn't agree with experiment, it's wrong."

"Nature uses only the longest threads to weave her patterns, so that each small piece of her fabric reveals the organization of the entire tapestry."

"Poets say science takes away from the beauty of the stars—mere globs of gas atoms. I, too, can see the stars on a desert night, and feel them. But do I see less or more?"

"Scientific views end in awe and mystery, lost at the edge in uncertainty, but they appear to be so deep and so impressive that the theory that it is all arranged as a stage for God to watch man's struggle for good and evil seems inadequate."

"The first principle is that you must not fool yourself, and you are the easiest person to fool."

"There is a computer disease that anybody who works with computers knows about. It's a very serious disease, and it interferes completely with the work. The trouble with computers is that you 'play' with them!"

"We are at the very beginning of time for the human race. It is not unreasonable that we grapple with problems. But there are tens of thousands of years in the future. Our responsibility is to do what we can, learn what we can, improve the solutions, and pass them on."

Carl Sagan:
"A celibate clergy is an especially good idea, because it tends to suppress any hereditary propensity toward fanaticism."

"For small creatures such as we, the vastness is bearable only through love."

"Imagination will often carry us to worlds that never were. But without it we go nowhere."

"In order to make an apple pie from scratch, you must first create the universe."

"It is of interest to note that while some dolphins are reported to have learned English (up to fifty words used in correct context), no human being has been reported to have learned dolphinese."

"Personally, I would be delighted if there were a life after death, especially if it permitted me to continue to learn about this world and others, if it gave me a chance to discover how history turns out."

"Somewhere, something incredible is waiting to be known."

"Skeptical scrutiny is the means, in both science and religion, by which deep thoughts can be winnowed from deep nonsense."

"The brain is like a muscle. When it is in use, we feel very good. Understanding is joyous."

"The universe seems neither benign nor hostile, merely indifferent."

"There are many hypotheses in science which are wrong. That's perfectly all right; they're the aperture to finding out what's right. Science is a self-correcting process. To be accepted, new ideas must survive the most rigorous standards of evidence and scrutiny."

"When you make the finding yourself—even if you're the last person on Earth to see the light—you'll never forget it."

When I was in high school, I knew a student who fit this profile very well. His name was Clifford (I will not use his last name, because he is out there somewhere—so Clifford, if you read this, please know I remember you vividly. And I still want to know what you wrote in my yearbook in Ancient Greek!). Clifford kept in the background and did not interact with the rest of us. He was so intelligent and smart that we could not even grasp a fraction of the workings of his mind. I recognized that he lived in a realm of imagination and possibilities where none of us could follow. Being an INFP myself, I recognized a fellow internal imaginative person, but I was not in his intellectual league; I *felt,* whereas he *thought.* He was extremely quiet and reserved. He was a visionary who kept his visions to himself—at least at that time, at least to us. I just know that he found other Submersibles to share his amazing insights with and is happily living in the depths of his wonderful and creative abilities.

Careers in which you are likely to find Submersibles would be philosophers (therefore, college campuses), scientists, physicists, mathematicians, medical researchers, scholars, software engineers, researchers, or astronomers. You will find that you do not actually know many Submersibles, because they tend to work best alone and do not interact with other employees that well, or often. Like the true submersible that represents their personality style, their work stations are limited and confined, only allowing necessary individuals into their territory. They are made to explore the deepest regions of our lives with their incredible curiosity, imagination, and drive. You will hear them saying "Why?" or Why not?" a lot.

Submersibles tend to "hang out" only with other Submersibles. They do not have a lot of patience or understanding for some of the other types, especially ones who are not comfortable with abstract conceptualizing; an example would be the Sensing types. Sensing types are concrete thinkers; they focus on the observable, the facts, the details; they are guided by past experience, whereas the Intuition part of the Submersible tends to ignore those things. Instead, they use their imagination, inspiration, and connections; they are interested in the bigger picture, the future possibility. A Submersible does not really care what *is;* they want to know what *could be.* Since a Submersible spends so much time in the deep, the details and facts of a normal, everyday world are beyond their radar.

If you are in a relationship with a Submersible, it can be a fulfilling life for you. Because Submersibles spend much of their time deeply involved in working internally, they tend to be quite uncomplicated, simplistic, and straightforward in their relationships. Since they are very creative and imaginative, they can bring a lot of originality and excitement to the relationship. The problem will come because they are so imaginative that their expectations can be greater than the reality of the relationship. So if you really want to keep that Submersible happy, you will need to be creative and imaginative yourself in order to meet those expectations. You will also need to be able to spend time alone, because they do get caught up in projects, ideas, and possibilities and forget that there is an everyday world that exists.

What a Submersible needs from you:

- Respect their privacy.

- Allow them to be independent and to spend time alone.

- Be interested in their creativity.

- Don't be upset with their messiness.

- Give them time to think things through.

If you are involved with a Submersible and you notice that they are becoming preoccupied with minor problems or becoming hypersensitive to others, then you are know that they are becoming overwhelmed. To get them back on track, it is helpful to ask them to join you in an activity; they need to be able to connect to their feelings at this time.

If you are a Submersible and experiencing difficulties because of your personality style, here are some suggestions:

- Admit that you are not a "feeling" person, but notice how people who are in relationships act toward each other.

- Allow yourself to really listen to other people, and try to understand their point of view.

- Consider the impact of your actions on others.

- Try to imagine the people in your life, and visualize what each person is doing and thinking—without judging whatever it is you imagine. Let the world in.

- Learn to relax. Be aware of the non-stop commentary occurring in your head.

Exercises that may be helpful:

- Keep a daily journal. Take a certain time each day to stop and notice the world around you. Notice the objects in your home, the colors; notice the plant life outside. Make it a habit whenever you go places to stop, get out of your head, and notice the world around you.

- Whenever you are with other people, make a concentrated effort to talk to them about something besides your specific area if interest. How do you feel when you talk about something that is not your preferred topic?

During a crisis situation, a Submersible will attempt to submerge even deeper into the realms of their magnificent possibilities, but this is a time when helping them connect with the people whom they love becomes important. It is a time when connection to others can add a dimension to their lives that was previously missing.

Submersibles tend to find spirituality through an approach of questioning and research. Mainly Submersibles will develop a private approach to their own spirituality that they have adapted from their various researches and studies. They will tend to have many books on the subject and, if they are really interested, will attend workshops or take classes. As they approach true spirituality, they directly experience an underlying connection with life, with everything around them. This connection, this ability to see the impermanence of life, creates a true compassion where they are able to share with others from the depths of their hearts.

"I am thankful for

My skepticism, which for me is a tool for getting at truth
My love of wrestling with complex issues, which challenge and
exercise my intellect
My curiosity that propels my search for truth
My understanding of the principles that regulate the universe

In the storms of my life, I can find shelter by

Focusing on the big picture and looking for new possibilities
Using others as a sounding board to clarify my values
Assessing the impact of the situation on those around me

To honor myself and my pathway to God, I can

Pursue and analyze those areas where I doubt
Honor my need for precision, enlightenment, and wholeness
Explore the ways my soulwork can benefit my relationships with
others" *Soul Types*, page 233

INTP Prayer: God, help me to be less independent, but let me do it
my way.

With practice, you will be more in tune with your own personal boat style, and also in assessing the people in your life. This will help you in your ability to have a better understanding of how they affect and fit into your life.

ESTP—RUNABOUT	(exciting, action, observant, goal-oriented)
ISTP—KAYAK	(independent, loners, risk-takers)
ESFP—CRUISE SHIP	(large groups, outgoing, pleasure)
ISFP—RAFT	(free thinker, sensual, sensitive)
ESTJ—PATROL BOAT	(stable, want things done their way)
ISTJ—CANOE	(simplicity, individualistic, quiet, natural)
ESFJ—CARGO SHIP	(dependable, hardworking, caretaker)
ISFJ—TUGBOAT	(respectful, responsible, full of warmth)
ENFJ—CABIN CRUISER	(pleasure, entertaining, security, flexible)
INFJ—SUBMARINE	(secretive, low profile, silent, caring)
ENFP—CATAMARAN	(novel, unique, spontaneous, caring)
INFP—NAUTILUS	(romantic, passionate, idealistic)
ENTJ—AIRCRAFT CARRIER	(analytical, organized, structured)
INTJ—SAILBOAT	(freedom, challenge, skill, pride)
ENTP—HOUSEBOAT	(comfort, mobility, variety)
INTP—SUBMERSIBLE	(creative, driven to understand)

Were you able to recognize yourself? How about the important people in your life?

Bibliography

Chapter 1, Types of Boats

Page 1, Myers-Briggs personality

page 1, Kiersey, David , *Please Understand Me II*, Prometheus Nemesis Book Company, 1998.

Page 1, Thompson, Lenore, *Personality Type: An Owner's Manual*, Shambhala, Boston and London, 1998.

page 9, Canfield, John, *Chicken Soup of the Soul*, *A Lesson In Heart* by Stan Frager

Chapter 2, SPs – Experiencers and Realists

page 29, Montgomery, Stephen, *The Pygmalion Project: Love and Coercion Among the Types. Volume One: The Artisian*, Prometheus Nemesis Book Company, 1989.

page 30 – RUNABOUT,

pages 32, Robin Williams, quotes from www.Thinkexist.com, and www.quotationspage.com

pages 32-33, Jim Carey quote about Carol Burnett, Jules Asner Host, *Revealed* Copyright © 2005 E! EntertainmentTelevision, Inc. direct quotes, www.thinkexist.com

page 33, Eddie Murphy, www.thinkexist.com

pages 33-34, Madonna, www.thinkexist.com

page 34, Lewis Carroll, *Alice In Wonderland*- page 37, Davich, Victor, *8 Minute Meditation,* A Perigee Book, New York, 2004.

Page 39, Hirsh, Sandra Krebs, and Kise, Jane A.G., *Soul Types; Finding the Spiritual Path That is Right For You,* Hyperion, New York, 1998, page 58. Link on internet

Page 40, KAYAK

page 41-42, Robert Redford, www.thinkexist,com, and www.goldenyears.org.

page 42, Charles Bronson

pages 42-43, James Dean
    American Legends : Janes Dean Rebel For All Seasons By Ron Martinetti

pages 43, Frank Zappa, to Baltimore Sun, Oct. 12, 1986
    ZAPPA - **(1940 - 1993)**, *Interview with this submitter, New York City, 5/08/1980*
    Hot Shot Digital Web Page Rock Tributes

page 44, WOODY ALLEN - Copyright © 2000-2002 by Film*Makers*.com.
    Film*Makers*.com is a division of Media Pro Tech Inc.

page 44-46, Amelia Earhart quotes, About : -- C.B. Allen, New York Herald Tribune, Fred Noonan, Amelia's navigator for the around-the-world flight, Walter J. Boyne

page 50-51, Hirsh, Sandra Krebs, and Kise, Jane A.G., *Soul Types; Finding the Spiritual Path That is Right For You,* Hyperion, New York, 1998., pg.218

Page 52 CRUISE SHIP

page 53-54, Elvis Presley, www.thinkexist.com

page 54-55, Reagan, Ronald

INDIANA UNIVERSITY
Quality Education. Lifetime Opportunities.

107 S. Indiana Ave. Bloomington, IN 47405-7000
812-856-3342

Last updated: June 8, 2004
www.thinkexist.com
page 56, MAGIC JOHNSON
Stars of Today Legends of yesterday
National Sports Agency
NBA@NationalSportsAgency.com
www.thinkexist.com
page 57, Goldie Hawn Copyright 1996-2005, IGN Entertainment,
Inc.
pages 61-62, Hirsh, Sandra Krebs, and Kise, Jane A.G., *Soul Types;
Finding the Spiritual Path That is Right For You*, Hyperion,
New York, 1998., page 73

RAFT - Page 63
page 65, Pauly Shore TIMELINE written by Justin
http://www.mutantreviewers.com/rtimepauly.html
The Rise and Fall of Mr. Pauly Shore
page 65, Phoebe – from "Friends" quotes
pages 66-67, Brigette Bardot Desperately Seeking Saison: A Love
Potion to Savour by Rich Rabassa and Ale Clayson Membre
de ClickFR, Reseau francophone Paie-Par-Click Geocities
www.thinkexist.com
pages 67-68, Paul McCartney
Quotes Page www.thinkexist.com
Song Quotes
Maybe I'm Amazed Lyrics
page 68, Doris Day, www.thinkexist.com
page 68, Liberace, www.brainyquotes.com
page 69, Elizabeth Taylor, www.thinkexist.com
page 69-70, Marilyn Monroe, www.thinkexist.com
page 70, Cher, www.thinkexist.com

page 74, Hirsh, Sandra Krebs, and Kise, Jane A.G., *Soul Types; Finding the Spiritual Path That is Right For You*, Hyperion, New York, 1998., page 285

CHAPTER 5 - SJs – Traditionalists

page 75, Kiersey, David, *Please Understand Me II*, Prometheus Nemesis Book Company, 1998.

page 75, Tieger, Paul D. and Barron-Tieger, Barbara, *Just Your Type*, Little, Brown and Company, Boston, New York, London, 2000.

page 76, Montgomery, Stephen, *The Pygmalion Project: Love and Coercion Among the Types. Volume Two: The Guardian*, Prometheus Nemesis Book Company, 1990.

ROWBOATS –

page 78, Lucy of *Peanuts*

page 78-80, Bette Davis Meeting Miss Davis, by Jim Emerson

page 80-82, John Wayne, www.thinkexist.com

page 82-83, Barbara Stanwyck
    Barbara Stanwyck: Working Girl, Movie Star **By** Jim Emerson

page 83, Bruce Willis, www.thinkexist.com

page 84, Raymond Burr, www.thinkexist.com

Page 88, Hirsh, Sandra Krebs, and Kise, Jane A.G., *Soul Types; Finding the Spiritual Path That is Right For You*, Hyperion, New York, 1998., page 187-188

CANOE

page 91, President George H.W. Bush, www.quotemonk.com

page 91, Evander Holyfield, www.thinkexist.com

pages 92, Julia Roberts, www.thinkexist.com

page 92-93, Gary Sinise, www.thinkexist.com

page 93, Kirk Douglas, www.thinkexist.com

page 93, Joe Friday from *Dragnet*

page 97-98, Hirsh, Sandra Krebs, and Kise, Jane A.G., *Soul Types; Finding the Spiritual Path That is Right For You*, Hyperion, New York, 1998.,page 87

CARGO SHIP
page 101, Mary Tyler Moore
Mary Tyler Moore interview by Chet Cooper
CONTINUED ABILITY MAGAZINE
page 102, Dixie Carter, www.thinkexist.com
page 102, Sally Field, www.thinkexist.com
page 102, Dr. Leonard McCoy – Star Trek bbc.co.uk
page 106, Hirsh, Sandra Krebs, and Kise, Jane A.G., *Soul Types;*
Finding the Spiritual Path That is Right For You, Hyperion,
New York, 1998., page 255.

TUG BOAT
page 108, Montgomery, Stephen, *The Pygmalion Project: Love and*
Coercion Among the Types. Volume Two: The Guardian,
Prometheus Nemesis Book Company, 1990., pg. 25
page, 109, Jimmy Stewart, www.thinkexist.com
page 109, Johnny Carson, www.thinkexist.com
page 109, Jerry Seinfeld, www.thinkexist.com
page 109-110, Tyne Daly, www.thinkexist.com
page 114, Hirsh, Sandra Krebs, and Kise, Jane A.G., *Soul Types;*
Finding the Spiritual Path That is Right For You, Hyperion,
New York, 1998., pg. 270

CHAPTER 6 IDEALISTS - PAGE 115
Page, 117, Choiniere, Ray, and Kiersey, David, *Presidential*
Temperament, Prometheus Nemesis Book Company, 1992.
page 493

CABIN CRUISERS
pages 119, Michael Jordan, www.thinkexist.com
pages 120, Oprah Winfrey, www.thinkexist.com
page 120-121, Diane Sawyer, www.thinkexist.com
page 121, Dick Van Dyke, www.thinkexist.com
page 121-122, John Denver
page 122 – John Denver Thompson, Lenore, *Personality Type: An*
Owner's Manual, Shambhala, Boston and London, 1998.,
pg. 359

pages 125, Hirsh, Sandra Krebs, and Kise, Jane A.G., *Soul Types;*
Finding the Spiritual Path That is Right For You, Hyperion,
New York, 1998 pg. 270

SUBMARINE -
pages 127, *FISTFUL OF DOLLARS*: The Man with No Name
"A Fistful of Dollars" Video Case Cover Information:
page 128, Batman – reference to
page 128, Shirley McClain
MacLaine, Shirley, *The Camino,* Pocket Books, New York,
2000., pages 217-218
page 128-129, Michael Landon
Carol (Channah Leah) Shoemaker TJones2020@aol.com
page, 128, *Conversations with Michael Landon* by Tom Ito(1992)
page 128-129, www.thinkexist.com
page 129, Carrie Fisher, www.thinkexist.com
pages 129-130, Nelson Mandela, www.brainyquote.com
page 133, Hirsh, Sandra Krebs, and Kise, Jane A.G., *Soul Types;*
Finding the Spiritual Path That is Right For You, Hyperion,
New York, 1998 pg. 165

CATAMARAN
Page 134, Picture of Ellips, http://www.paritetboat.com/
page 135-136, Andy Rooney
"A Few Minutes with Andy Rooney," CBS
www.thinkexist.com
page 136, Paul Harvey
KLMJ-FM Paul Harvey Advertisement Page
www.thinkexist.com
page 136-137, Carol Burnett, www.thinkexist.com
page 137, Martin Short, www.thinkexist.com
page 137, Meg Ryan, www.thinkexist.com
page 137-138, Sandra Bullock
page 137 - **by Bob Strauss**
Terms of Use. Copyright © 2005 E! Entertainment
Television, Inc. All rights reserved.
page 137-138, www.thinkexist.com
page 138-139, Ariel from *The Little Mermaid*– by DISNEY movie

page 143-144, Hirsh, Sandra Krebs, and Kise, Jane A.G., *Soul Types; Finding the Spiritual Path That is Right For You*, Hyperion, New York, 1998 – page 137

NAUTILIS
Page 145, Drawing of Nautilis courtesy of Ron Miller, Illlustrator
page 146, Verne, Jules, *Twenty Thousand Leagues Under the Sea*, Barnes & Noble Classics, Pages 77-78,
Page 146 , *Twenty Thousand leagues Under The Sea, Barnes & Noble Classics*, page 73
pages 148-149, Isabelle Briggs Myers
    CAPT – Center for Applications of Psychological type
    info@capt.org
Page 149-150, Carl Jung, www.thinkexist.com and
    www. Brainyquote.com
page 151-152, James Taylor Lyrics, www.stylrics.rare_lyrics.com/
    songs/jamestaylor1976.html
pages 152-153, Carl Rogers, www.thinkexist.com
page 153-154, Neil Diamond, www.lyrics.rare_lyrics.com/N/Neil-
    Diamond.html
page 154-155, Princess Diana, www.thinkexist.com
page 156, Jim Croce, Lyrics – www.twin-musiclyrics
page 157, Deanna Troi – STAR TREK, www.tvsothertenpercent.
    tripod.com/startrek/troi.html
page 158-159, Bill Watterson, author of *Calvin and Hobbes*
page 158, *CALVIN and Hobbes* by Bill Waterson
    CALVIN' CREATOR'S SECRET HIDEOUT'
    CARTOONIST BILL WATTERSON RETURNS TO A
    CLOISTERED LIFE
    The Plain Dealer; Cleveland, OH; Dec 20, 1998;
    JOHN C. KUEHNER PLAIN DEALER REPORTER;
    (Copyright (c) The Plain Dealer 1998)
Page 158-159, Calvin and Hobbes quotes, www.
    homepage,eircom.net~odyssey/quotes/popular/comics/
    Calvin_Hobbes.html

pages 163-164, Hirsh, Sandra Krebs, and Kise, Jane A.G., *Soul Types; Finding the Spiritual Path That is Right For You*, Hyperion, New York, 1998 pg. 300

CHAPTER 7 Rationals

AIRCRAFT CARRIER
page 168, General George Patton,
www.generalpatton.com/quotes.html
page 169, Newt Gingrich, www.thinkexist.com
page 169-170, Napoleon, www.thinkexist.com
page 170-171, Margaret Thatcher, www.thinkexist.com
page 171, Steve Martin, www.thinkexist.com
page 175-176, Hirsh, Sandra Krebs, and Kise, Jane A.G., *Soul Types; Finding the Spiritual Path That is Right For You*, Hyperion, New York, 1998 pg. 203

SAILBOATS
page 178, TV show *HOME IMPROVEMENT* - "Wilson" reference
pages 179-180, Katherine Hepburn
  TRIBUTE TO Katharine Hepburn
  Special Thoughts for FILMS FOR TWO
  by Sharon Levine Waldman
Page 180, www.thinkexist.com
page 180, Phil Donahue
  MSNBC quote – regarding new show
  www.thinkexist.com
page 181, Chevy Chase
  AMCTV.com
  page 217, *From Laker Jim's Fletch Won Interviews with Tim Mateson*
  www.thinkexist.com
page 181-182, Clarice Starling
  Thomas, Harris, *HANNIBAL LECTRE* and *SILENCE OF THE LAMBS*
Page 185-186, Hirsh, Sandra Krebs, and Kise, Jane A.G., *Soul Types; Finding the Spiritual Path That is Right For You*, Hyperion, New York, 1998, page 151

HOUSEBOAT
page 188, Steven Spielberg, www.thinkexist.com
page 189, Leonardo Davinci, www.brainyquotes.com
page 190, Walt Disney, www.brainyquotes.com
page 190, Tom Hanks, www.brainyquotes
page 191, Wile E Coyote – Looney Tunes
page 194-195, Hirsh, Sandra Krebs, and Kise, Jane A.G., *Soul Types; Finding the Spiritual Path That is Right For You*, Hyperion, New York, 1998 pg. 122

SUBMERSIBLE
page 197-198, Albert Einstein, www.quotesoftheheart.com
page 198, www.aip.org/history/einstein
page 198, Bob Newhart, www.thinkexist.com
page 198, Rick Moranis, Comedian Under Glass
        Starlog August 1989 #145
        By: Jami Bernard
page 198-199, Stephen Hawking, www.thinkexist.com
page 200-201, Richard Feynman, www.thinkexist.com
page 201-202, Carl Sagan, www.thinkexist.com
page 205-206, Hirsh, Sandra Krebs, and Kise, Jane A.G., *Soul Types; Finding the Spiritual Path That is Right For You*, Hyperion, New York, 1998 - pg. 233